Doing Gender in

MW00513775

Exploring the relationship between gender and events, this book delivers an ethnographic analysis of the celebration of gender equality in the context of the culture-led event. Drawing upon Critical Event Studies, Anthropology of the Festive and Gender Studies, this book provides a comprehensive understanding of the entangled, conceptual entities of gender and events.

Through a gendered analysis of the culture-led event, *Hull UK City of Culture 2017*, this work expands epistemological perspectives relevant to the study of events in general and City/Capital of Culture initiatives in particular. Driven by a feminist, collaborative methodological approach, the book draws on four years of ethnographic, qualitative research in the city of Hull and its celebration of the title, UK City of Culture in 2017 and provides an in-depth analysis of how audiences engage, performances enact, and infrastructures condition the production of cultures of gender equality in the citywide celebration.

This will be a valuable resource for upper-level students and academics in the field of Event Studies, Cultural Policy, Geography, Anthropology and Gender Studies.

Barbara Grabher is a trained Anthropologist working on the intersections of Gender, Urban and Critical Event Studies. She currently works as a postdoctoral researcher in the Institute of Geography and Regional Sciences at the University of Graz, Austria. Prior to this position, she was employed as research assistant in the Culture, Place and Policy Institute at the University of Hull, UK, where she contributed to the final evaluation study of Hull UK City of Culture 2017, focusing on the impact area, Society and Wellbeing. In 2020, Barbara completed her PhD at the University of Hull and University of Oviedo, Spain. She holds a BA in Cultural and Social Anthropology from the University of Vienna, Austria, and an MA in Gender Studies from Utrecht University, the Netherlands and the University of Granada, Spain.

Routledge Critical Event Studies Research Series
Edited by Rebecca Finkel, *Queen Margaret University, UK*, and David McGillivray, *University of the West of Scotland, UK*

Gendered Violence at International Festivals
An Interdisciplinary Perspective
Edited by Louise Platt and Rebecca Finkel

Events and Well-being
Edited by Allan Stewart Jepson and Trudie Walters

Doing Gender in Events
Feminist Perspectives in Critical Event Studies
Barbara Grabher

For more information about this series, please visit: www.routledge.com/tourism/series/RCE

Doing Gender in Events
Feminist Perspectives in Critical
Event Studies

Barbara Grabher

Routledge
Taylor & Francis Group

LONDON AND NEW YORK

First published 2022
by Routledge
2 Park Square, Milton Park, Abingdon, Oxon OX14 4RN

and by Routledge
605 Third Avenue, New York, NY 10158

Routledge is an imprint of the Taylor & Francis Group, an informa business

© 2022 Barbara Grabher

British Library Cataloguing-in-Publication Data
A catalogue record for this book is available from the British Library

Library of Congress Cataloging-in-Publication Data
A catalog record has been requested for this book

ISBN: 978-0-367-63975-4 (hbk)
ISBN: 978-0-367-63976-1 (pbk)
ISBN: 978-1-003-12160-2 (ebk)

DOI: 10.4324/9781003121602

Typeset in Times New Roman
by Newgen Publishing UK

To my parents

Contents

Illustrations

Figure

Tables

Acknowledgements

This book would not have been possible without the research participants' contributions to the project: *Gendering Cities of Culture*. I explicitly thank the team of observing-participants for gifting me their time, thoughts and reflections for the purpose of this analysis.

As this book is based on my doctoral research project, my sincere gratitude goes to my supervisors, Dr Josef Ploner and Professor Suzanne Clisby, who accompanied me in my investigative process. Their insightful comments, encouraging words and challenging questions were highly appreciated. I would like to thank the editors of this book series, Dr Rebecca Finkel and Professor David McGillivray, for their feedback and support. Many thanks as well to Lydia Kessell and Emma Travis at Routledge for their help. Thanks to Dr Janine Hatter, Dr Jennifer Jones, Dr Doris Pany-Habsa and my fellow writers in Hull and Graz; I have learned that writing does not need to be a lonely task. Thank you for your mentorship, thorough proof reading and continuous motivation in the process of crafting this book. Special thanks go to Dr Enrico Tommarchi and Dr Alexandra Oancă, who gave detailed feedback on the full draft of this book. I am very grateful for the continuous exchange and their collegiality.

Over the past five years, I have had the opportunity to work with many colleagues in different academic settings. Thus, I would like to mention the team of researchers on the GRACE Project, who created a nurturing environment in which to learn and develop as a scholar and human being. Further, I would like to thank Professor Franco Bianchini and the team at the Culture, Place and Policy Institute. As informal advisors and later co-workers, I am grateful to have studied and researched in this centre of knowledge on urban, culture-led regeneration at University of Hull. Finally, I would like to express my gratitude to my current team led by Professor Anke Strüver at University of Graz. Their motivational messages, curious questions and helpful advice were highly appreciated in the final editing process.

I am very grateful for my family and friends, who repeatedly remind me to balance work and life in order to ensure a healthy writing process and experience. Particularly, I would like to thank my parents for encouraging me to always stay curious and determined to achieve my ambitions. Danke.

This project received funding from the European Union's Horizon 2020 research and innovation programme under the Marie Skłodowska-Curie grant agreement No 675378.

Abbreviations

BP	British Petroleum
COC	City/Capital of Culture
ECOC	European Capital of Culture
Hull 2017 Ltd	Hull UK City of Culture 2017 Limited
Hull2017	Hull UK City of Culture 2017
LGBT+	Umbrella term to describe sexual and gender identities including, among others, Lesbian, Gay, Bisexual, Transgender, Intersex, Queer/Questioning, Asexual, Nonbinary, Pansexual.
LGBT50	Name of the commemorative event in celebration of the 50th anniversary of the partial decriminalisation of homosexuality in England and Wales.
UKCOC	UK City of Culture
UKIP	United Kingdom Independence Party

1 Relating gender and events
An introduction

Rationale, aim and structure

An explosion of confetti inspires this book. In the midst of my ethno-graphic fieldwork in 2017 during Hull's celebration of the title *UK City of Culture*,[1] I was showered with the colourful snippets of paper at the end of the *LGBT50* celebrations. Commemorating the 50th anniver-sary of the partial decriminalisation of homosexuality in England and Wales, the symbol of joy was catapulted into the air in order to make its slow dance back towards the ground. The metaphorical experience deeply moved me and, ever since, guides my thinking about the rela-tionship between celebratory events, the negotiations of socio-cultural values and the related potential for cultures of gender equality.

The aim of this book is to imbricate the notions of gender and events. Through a lens of Critical Event Studies, I discuss the interrelations of the two subjects. While events are addressed extensively from an operational, managerial perspective, my conceptualisations are guided by the political relevance of celebrations: I understand events as defined by their socio-cultural significance, characterised through a strong ethos of transformation and therefore acting as tools for meaning-making. On the basis of this interpretation, I am interested to interrogate how events correlate with the ambition for cultures of gender equality.

While I refer to a variety of events in order to illustrate the concep-tual discussions of gender-sensitive event studies, my analysis focuses on the celebration of *Hull UK City of Culture 2017*[2] and its acclaimed "365 days of transformative culture" (Hull 2017 Ltd, 2015: 14). On the one hand, I reason this empirical concentration on a single case study through the European Commission's (2009) claim that the independ-ence of host cities is a crucial success factor for City/Capital of Culture[3] initiatives. While trends, developments and best practice models have

DOI: 10.4324/9781003121602-1

shaped COC frameworks, the particular events are supposed to respond to local, urban needs:

> Like a living organism, the event is forever evolving and developing. [...] Geography, history, a country's size, politics, budgets, the cultural scene, the men and women on the board of the project and those organising its artistic side, all mix up into a different cocktail of distinct flavours.
>
> (European Commission 2009: 3–4)

On the other hand, I argue that an analytical focus on a singular case study is necessary as the negotiation of socio-cultural values is highly context sensitive (Grabher, 2019). In order to do justice to the particular local, regional and national interpretations of gender equality, I provide an in-depth analysis of the specificities that contributed to the negotiation of cultures of gender equality in Hull2017. This does not reduce the empirical discussions of this book to the mere context of Hull or the 2017 UKCOC event. As outlined in the final chapter, I envision the detailed insights into Hull2017 to serve as crucial points of departure for further explorations of other events, frameworks and localities.

How to navigate this book

Including this introduction, the book is structured in six chapters. While the chapters build on each other conceptually as well as empirically they can be read as individual sections as they interrogate selected questions on their own. Therefore, the following research queries are addressed in the further chapter discussions:

1 *(Extended) Introduction*: How are cultures of gender equality produced in events?
2 *Reprogramming transformative ambitions*: How are transformative ambitions engrained in the City/Capital of Culture event framework?
3 *Engagements through equality*: How are audiences engaging with produced cultures of gender equality in the context of *Hull2017*?
4 *Performance, events and equality*: How are cultures of gender equality performed through the programmed activities of *Hull2017*?
5 *Equality in structure*: What kind of infrastructural arrangements accommodate the production of cultures of gender equality in the context of *Hull2017*?

In addition to the chapters and their guiding questions, I summarise the discussions and provide readers with an outlook and invitation for further research in the final chapter of this book.

Relating gender and events – an introduction

Through a conceptual unfolding, this introductory chapter presents the relationship of gender and events. I discuss the term 'event' and highlight the developments of the contemporary industry sector and related research field. Beyond the current and mainstream investigative agenda of Event Studies, I situate my research in the emerging canons of Critical Event Studies, foregrounding the interest in the political potential of events and the socio-cultural significance of celebrations. Similar to the discussions regarding the notion of events, I address the terms 'gender' and 'gender equality'. With reference to various celebrations, I highlight the marginalised, but existing gender-sensitive approaches in Event Studies. In a concise synopsis, I finalise the introduction by emphasising that events are tools for meaning-making and therefore require a reading of the "party" in relation to "its politics" (Browne, 2007: 63).

Reprogramming transformative ambitions – observations of shifting ambitions in city/capital of culture initiatives

Encompassing discussions of the research methodology and field conditions, the second chapter presents the case study of Hull2017 in respect to its developments and relevance for the study of gender and events. The slogan, *Change Is Happening*, by Hull-based developers Wykeland, characterises the atmosphere of Hull as UKCOC in 2017. Relating Hull's celebration to examples such as Derry/Londonderry, UKCOC in 2013, as well as Donostia/San Sebastián, *European Capital of Culture*[4] in 2017, I address the COC frameworks through an ongoing "(re)programming" (Immler and Sakkers, 2014: 22) trend. As aims and ambitions of host cities are steadily changing, I highlight how cultural transformations are embraced within the COC framework. These considerations serve as a point of departure for my gender-sensitive analysis of Hull's celebration.

Engagements through equality – studying encounters and dynamics of audiences in equality-themed events

Following the conceptual and methodological introductions, the third chapter serves as the first of three analytical chapters. Here, I highlight how audiences engage with cultures of gender equality in the context of Hull's celebration. On the basis of my analysis, I argue that event experiences not only shape the individual and collective interpretations of equality, but also the event and its narrative as a whole. The analysis highlights two key themes: Firstly, I interrogate how participants encounter cultures of gender equality in the celebratory context. Secondly, in order to understand the audience dynamics in the celebration of equality, I counterbalance sensations of togetherness and strategies of inclusion with experiences of echo chambers and exclusion. I end the chapter in discussion of the sustainability of the engagements with equality in event settings and, in the words of a research participant, highlight the need to continue the conversation.

Performance, events and equality – examining the production of cultures of gender equality in the performed contents of events

In the fourth chapter, I outline how selected equality-themed activities in Hull2017 perform cultures of gender equality. The meaning-making practices of events are crucial conceptual influences in this analytical discussion. Focusing on six events, I highlight differing – at times even conflicting – interpretations of equality. Hence, I conclude that cultures of gender equality are multi-layered and therefore celebrated in their plurality in the context of its celebration in a COC event. Supported by this conceptual understanding, I argue that events serve as particularly useful platforms to negotiate this plurality of meanings. Through my narrative analysis, I explore what and how stories of equality are being told. Additionally, my focus lies on the performers, as I ask who is responsible for the production of equality and query why artists and producers are drawn to this duty.

Equality in structure – investigating infrastructural conditions and the production of cultures of gender equality

Guided by research participants' observations, the fifth chapter concentrates on the infrastructural conditions of events. In my analysis, I point out the importance of this analytical perspective, as these structural levels strongly affect the meaning-making potential of events as socio-cultural values of gender equality are either supported or harmed by these infrastructural conditions. Among a vast number of structural influences, I concentrate on three dominant themes and therefore focus on the festivalisation, the material conditions and the commodification of equality. Provocatively, I ask, So what?, and argue that for the celebration of equality, further attention needs to be paid to these event infrastructures.

Doing gender in events – perspectives for an eventful future

In the final chapter, I summarise and reflect on the conceptual, methodological and analytical discussions regarding the imbrications of gender and events. Following the synopsis, the chapter provides recommendations for future research in accordance with learnings provided in the previous chapters. Thus, I, firstly, call for further research on the relationship between gender and events and strongly encourage investigative enquiries of events, which do not associate with gender-sensitive contents, structures or ambitions. Secondly, in reflection of my own analytical encounter with the infrastructural conditions of events, I outline the need for a critical study of these structural levels in order to advance debates regarding the meaning-making practices of events. I close the chapter and the book in acknowledging the drastic changes of the event landscape due to the COVID-19 pandemic and highlight that even in the absence of physical events, critical research is required to understand the relevance of events as tools for meaning-making in contemporary societies.

What are events? Grasping developments, concepts and ideas

In the following introductory discussion, I enter the conceptual debate of the notions of gender and events. I, firstly, discuss the term 'event' and explore the social and cultural practice of celebration as an experience-based condition. Secondly, I outline the existent synergies between gender and events. Thus, I highlight examples of gender-sensitive Event Studies and consider how gender is lived, politicised and imagined in the context of celebrations. This discussion leads me to argue that events are tools for meaning-making.

The notion 'event' carries a plurality of meanings, which is influenced by the colloquial usage of the term in various contexts. In this book, I use 'event' as a generic notion to refer to the investigated phenomenon and regularly substitute the term for other generic notions such as 'activity', 'festival' or 'celebration'. These variations are based on a stylistic choice and grounded in the anthropological roots of the studied subject, as discussed below. While their generic nature allows a – somewhat – interchangeable use, the term 'event' requires further definition.

Capturing the notion of 'events', I refer to Getz's (2007: 9) compositional term "planned events". Colloquially referred to as "remarkable occurrence", planned events are "an experience that has been designed (or at least the experience is facilitated) and would not otherwise occur" (Getz, 2007: 9). While this definition is useful as a working terminology for my purposes, I distance myself from the usage of the word 'planned' as a descriptor of events. This attribution serves to distinguish 'planned events' from other type of 'accidental' events, which might be caused by personal traumas, natural disasters or political conflicts. While I acknowledge the necessary distinction, I consider the attribution 'planned' misleading, erasing or diminishing the broad experiential spectrum, which I aim to capture in my ethnographic research of events. In order to grant space to the crucial sensations of surprise and immediacy in events (E. Turner, 2012), I work with Getz's (2007) definition of events but drop the term 'planned'.

Furthermore, the canons of Event Studies use a variety of attributes to emphasise the purpose and size of an event. Terminologies such as "sporting events" (Finkel, 2015: 218) or "combined arts events" (Finkel, 2009: 3) characterise events in reference to their key purpose. While this research focuses on activities, which could be categorised as 'combined arts events', I find this categorisation arbitrary for the aim of this study. Rather than referring to their purpose, the thematic interests of the investigated events are of greater value to my study. Therefore, I describe the selected activities as "equality-themed events" (Grabher, 2019: 14), in expression of the gender-sensitive and equality-provoking contents, structures or ambitions of the researched celebrations.[5] Additionally, due to strong interests in operational and managerial perspectives in Event Studies, events are frequently categorised in accordance to their scope and scale. Categories such as "mega-event", "hallmark event" or "special event" (Hall, 1989: 263) are used extensively as a reference to describe the costs and reach of events. While the investigated events of the UKCOC framework are mainly characterised as 'mega-event' or 'hallmark event', these operational categorisations are only of secondary interests to my qualitative research of the transformative potential of events for the production of cultures of gender equality. Therefore, I refer to the investigated celebration solely through the notion 'event' without adding further prefixes for an eventual categorisation of size, scale or scope.

Beyond definitions of the term 'event', the developments of the contemporary event industry and its research progressions situate the current practices and studies of the investigated activities. In the form of a procedural overview, Newbold et al. (2015) summarise the developments of the European event sector throughout the second half of the twentieth century. The scholars argue that in the 1940s and 1950s, events developed with explicit interest in art for art's sake. The following two decades were marked by an orientation towards the community. Thus, festivals became forums of political activism and symbolic resistance. Throughout the 1980s and 1990s, a radical transformation can be observed, as the formerly politically informed and fringe phenomenon faced commercialisation and commodification. Following Newbold et al.'s (2015) summary, Cudny (2016) synthesises that in this latest period, a festivalisation trend can be observed as events became an economic industry. With respect to the increasing presence of events in urban as well as rural schedules of activities, event-related research agendas have been established in response to the lucrative new industry sector. Strongly defined by managerial and touristic research interests, Event Studies were constituted as a field of study and even entered higher education curricula (Lamond and Platt, 2016).

While events and their study are strongly determined by operational research agendas, I am interested in the investigative approaches captured in the emerging subfield of Critical Event Studies. Newbold et al. (2015) recognise that disciplines such as Anthropology and Sociology pioneered the research canons of events. In the edited volume, *Time Out of Time*, Falassi (1987b) even goes as far as to acknowledge Goethe's descriptions of the Roman Carnival as one of the first ethnographic depictions of a celebration. He highlights Goethe's account not only as a narrative of "a pleasant spectacle, a joyful amusement, an aesthetic experience bringing exhilaration to the spirit", but to be an analysis of the festive as a "mirror of culture and a metaphor of life itself" (Falassi, 1987b: 14). While the origins of Event Studies are marginalised as footnotes in contemporary textbooks (Frost, 2015), investigations of the socio-cultural potential of events are experiencing a revival through Critical Event Studies research interests. Lamond and Platt (2016: 5) summarise:

> Critical Event Studies takes the concept of 'event', within the field of events studies, to be essentially contested. It does not shy away from that contestation – nor does it see contestation as a problem to be resolved – instead it recognises this essential contestation as a creative dynamic that powers and enhances research, and understanding, placing it at the forefront of our work as academics interested in events.

Within my own research, this approach grounds my conceptual interpretation of events as it enables me to understand its entanglements and developments with and through gender.

Events and their socio-cultural significance; or why events matter!

Falassi (1987a) understands celebrations as markers of society. According to the scholar, celebrations play with notions and values that societies and communities share. Therefore, he elucidates that "the primary and most general function of the festival is to renounce and then to announce culture" (Falassi, 1987a: 3). As ritualised acts, celebrations acknowledge transitions, reaffirm status and create moments of release. Therefore, celebrations hold the potential to engage, distort and express the zeitgeist of the location in which they are situated.

Following Falassi's (1987a) observation, Finkel (2015) reaffirms that events do not take place in a vacuum. Rather, celebrations are embedded in and expressive of their contemporary situatedness. In his analysis of the nineteenth-century *World Fairs* as mega-events of their time, Benedict (1983: 2) illustrates this interpretation, as he notes:

> The fairs were not only selling goods, they were selling ideas: ideas about the relations between nations, the spread of education, the advancement of science, the form of cities, the nature of domestic life, the place of art in society. They were presenting an ordered world. Many of these ideas could be seen in concrete (or at least plaster) forms at the expositions.

The reference to the "selling of ideas" exemplifies the conceptual understanding of celebrations and their socio-cultural significance. Events reproduce a monitored and artificial reality, which allows a close reading of desired local and temporal particularities, as several scholars outline.[6] Based on this interpretation, I understand events as techniques for the promotion of political ideologies, communal values, cultural assets and social dynamics that become meaningful through the concentrated spatiality and temporality of celebrations. Falassi (1987a: 2) summarises:

> Both the social function and the symbolic meaning of the festival are closely related to a series of overt values that the community recognizes as essential to its ideology and worldview, to its social identity, its historical continuity and to its physical survival, which is ultimately what the festival celebrates.

Therefore, I argue events are highly political, value-laden practices in intensified cultural and social circumstances.

Gender and cultures of equality – and what events have got to do with it

Next to the clarification of the notion of events and the related research developments, the subject of gender and the investigated cultures of gender equality require further attention. In the context of this book, I distance myself from a biological interpretation of sex and investigate instead gender as a product of socio-cultural norms. My analytical perspective is informed by the doing gender approach formulated by West and Zimmerman (1987). This analytical approach can be best summarised as an active doing, rather than a passive being of gender. Informed by social constructivist traditions, the scholars distinguish between the categories of sex and gender: While sex is assigned to bodies in respect to socio-cultural markers, gender is expressed through social interactions (Dashper and Finkel, 2020). As a modality of presentation and representation, individuals and communities negotiate the enactments of gender continuously. Therefore, my analysis is based on an understanding of gender as a daily practice, a social pattern of interactions, a complex power relationship. This interpretation of the term 'gender' does not reduce the notion merely to the categories of women or men – gender is much more than that! While these dual categories are an important part of the socio-cultural practice of gender, the doing gender approach enables me also to read practices of the deconstruction of gendered norms. Challenging the masculine status quo, questioning supposedly fixed assumptions about femininity or playing with the boundaries of gender binaries are crucial ways to understand the doing – or rather, undoing – of gender. It is crucial to note that as a social construct and practice, gender continuously intersects with other markers of identity, such as ethnicity or class among others (Holvino, 2010). Due to the context of my research, the intersecting practices of gender and sexuality are of particular relevance. As discussed in detail in the next section, this practice of doing gender – and sexuality – becomes particularly interesting in the context of events.

Furthermore, for the purpose of this research, I address the notion of gender equality as the core entity of this investigation. Related to the above discussed definition of gender as a socio-cultural practice and its intersectional correlations, I address gender equality as the aspired result of the ongoing feminist movements. Therefore, I do not address gender equality as a set of predefined parameters, but as a political process. Consequently, I research gender equality as a site of intervention rather than an established subject: gender equality as a practice and process of negotiation defines my research interest (Grabher, 2019). Even though I understand gender equality as a fluid process, the investigation of cultures of gender equality in the context of Hull2017 must be conceptualised within the parameters of the UK's Equality Act 2010. Described by the European Institute for Gender Equality (2021) as a "landmark piece of legislation that overrode all previous gender-equality laws for England, Scotland and Wales", the policy includes the Public Sector Equality Duties, which secures gender mainstreaming in the UK. This policy context shapes the investigated event of Hull2017. Therefore, I take the UK policy definitions of gender equality into consideration as an orientation but allow myself to read the process of negotiations of cultures of gender equality in events beyond the statutory acknowledgement.

Gendered events and eventful gender – research correlations and synergies

Pielichaty (2015: 237) highlights that "festivals are a significant site for the investigation of gender". In a similar vein, Coyle and Platt (2015: 275) declare: "Using festivit[ies] to champion a particular political viewpoint or as an act of collective activism is nothing new". Consequentially, the previously discussed socio-cultural significance of celebrations becomes tangible in the productions of cultures of gender equality in event settings.

While the cited scholars showcase the relationship between gender and events, Platt and Finkel (2018) clarify that the correlations between the two subjects are only just emerging. Goulding and Saren (2009) explain the limited history through the independent developments of the two research agendas: due to their simultaneously marginal positions within dominant disciplinary contexts, only recently have a growing number of studies embraced – either implicitly or explicitly – gender and events in relation to each other.

While the subject matter is limited in its extent and history, associated scholars continue to argue that celebrations illustrate in multiple ways imbrications with gender (Markwell and Waitt, 2013).[7] In its fairly recent history, a heightened attention in scholarly literature towards certain types of events can be observed. These celebrations are explicitly marked by their inscribed socio-cultural interests and related audiences. Consequently, LGBT+ events dominate the scholarly canons of gender-sensitive Event Studies. The main body of research in this area explores Pride parades and parties but expands into general considerations of LGBT-related event infrastructures.[8] Additionally, though they are numerically outnumbered, feminist festivals are under investigation by researchers (Coyle and Platt, 2015; Dashper and Finkel, 2020). Hereby, the *Michigan Womyn's Music Festival* has a crucial role in the debate: its size, popularity and controversies concerning access policies raised scholarly interest in the discussion of gender and festivals.[9] Events without an explicit gender- or sexuality-sensitive focus are hardly represented in the literature as sites for the production of gender.[10]

In order to further illustrate the conceptual entanglements between gender and events, I draw upon three analytical perspectives that shape the limited but existing literature. Thus, I align with suggestions contributed by Browne (2007), who proposes an analysis of the lived, politicised and imaginary potential of gender in events. Through local, national and international examples, I illustrate how a relational reading of the two concepts of gender and events can enable correlations and synergies.

Living gender through events

The socio-cultural significance of events is most immediate, visible and comprehensive through the lived experiences of gender and therefore constitutes the first and crucial analytical perspective. Markwell and Waitt (2013) point out that in the analysis of events, the celebratory community and its individuals may not be regarded as static entities: identities cannot be considered as pre-set; rather, festive events need to be addressed as a space-time, in which participants relate to and shape their identities. As celebrations invoke cultural meaning, personal perceptions and experiences are shaped through them.

Eder et al.'s (1995) research on women participating in the *Michigan Womyn's Music Festival* exemplifies this analytical perspective on the lived experiences of gender through events. The authors investigate the effects of participation in the festival on women's lives. Reflecting not only on participants' experiences on the festival grounds but relating these with their daily lives, many attendees described their participation as an escape from the conventions of mainstream culture. According to the participating women in Eder et al.'s (1995) study, the personal experience of the celebration creates an environment envisioned as a feminist utopia of emancipation, freedom and liberation. Even beyond the immediate event experience on the camp site, the authors note influences on the lived experiences of gender in the women's day to day life. Attentive to the further trajectories of participants, Eder et al. (1995) highlight that festival visitors narrate a sense of renewal due to the collective celebration – even beyond the temporally limited and spatially defined festival experiences. Therefore, according to Eder et al. (1995), beyond a mere interpretation of having a good time, the sensations of renewal and empowerment shape the lived notion of gender in the context of event experiences.

Beyond the personal relations and reflections, sensations of the community are noted by scholars as a form of living gender through events. Thus, researchers frequently refer to the conceptual notion of communitas put forward by Edith Turner (2012) and Victor Turner (1989).[11] In Eder et al.'s (1995) study, the collective notion of participation crucially influences the individual experiences. The authors suggest that in abstract or literal forms, participants in the *Michigan Womyn's Music Festival* build relationships with the celebratory community, which influence both their personal and collective experiences of gender through the event. Therefore, the socio-cultural significance of events is enacted as the lived experience of gender.

Gender-political event agendas

Incorporating considerations of the personal and collective experiences of gender in events, scholars furthermore address the relationship between gender-sensitive politics and celebrations. As addressed previously, Benedict (1983: 2) claims events are "selling ideas" and political agendas have shaped and continue to shape celebrations. Generally speaking, the temporal and spatial concentrations and linked high levels of visibility foster the political potential of events. Therefore, in their condensed format, events signal immediate, explicit political demands and affiliations (Ammaturo, 2016; Browne, 2007).

In her examination of the *Eurovision Song Contest*, Baker (2015, 2017, 2019) exemplifies this critical relationship between celebrations, gender and politics. While gender equality is not an official agenda of the music broadcasting event, Baker (2017) captures gender-political highlights of the contest throughout its history. The first openly gay and trans performers in 1997 and 1998, the premier same-sex kiss by the Russian duo t.A.T.u. in 2003 and the victory of the drag performer Conchita Wurst in 2014 are just a few examples of gender-political statements in the competition. On the basis of this observation, Baker (2017) argues that the event's developments of the 1990s and 2000s match several national and European discourses on the institutionalisation of gender and sexual equality. Consequentially, Baker (2017: 101–102) explains that "*Eurovision [Song Contest]* [...] entered a context where certain state governments and European institutions were constructing LGBT+ equality as a matter of European identity and national pride". Linked to Puar's (2013) notion of 'homonationalism',[12] Baker (2017) highlights that the popular culture event strongly relates to and expresses the political ambitions of constructing a European cultural citizenship. While spatial limitations of this book restrict a further debate on the concept of homonationalism and its enactment through events, Baker's (2015, 2017, 2019) discussion of the *Eurovision Song Contest* serves to illustrate how gender-sensitive politics are enacted through events.

Enabling alternative imaginations through events

Beyond the personal and political effects of events, various scholars[13] stress that celebrations are fertile grounds for imagining alternatives to the status quo. With strong links to Victor Turner's (1969, 1974, 1982, 1987a, 1987b, 1989) concept of liminality,[14] assumptions of transgressions continue to be an influential frame of analysis for events, festivals and celebrations (Grabher, 2020). Hahm et al. (2018) summarise celebrations as a process of raising awareness which allows for a potential exploration of imaginaries. The authors argue that, within events, the participants' individual consciousness is heightened by exposure to, exploration of and engagement with the wider community. The individual awareness therefore exists in relation to a collective perspective through moments of celebratory actions. According to Hahm et al.'s (2018) call for heightened awareness, events hold a great creative power for collective and individual imaginations.

In her auto-ethnographic study and queer reading of the *Wild Ginger Witch Camp*, Jones (2010) explores how an imaginary potential is engrained in events. As witchcraft and wicca culture is celebrated in the camp, she argues that the event is a materialisation of the imaginary shared by celebratory communities. The camp publicly manifests individual accounts and creates an identity of the celebratory community. Therefore, the event materialises a space-time in which boundaries of the imaginary might be enlarged, re-configured and adjusted. Though only temporary, the gathering creates an alternative space-time to the status quo, informing the imaginary of witchcraft and wicca culture.

These observations of celebrating the imaginary also find resonance in studies of LGBT+ Pride events by Pielichaty (2015), Browne (2007) and Kates (2003). Researching events in Dublin, Brighton or

Sydney, respectively, the scholars highlight that gender and sexuality is (de)constructed through the conditions that the festive event creates. Characterised through heightened awareness and liminal experiences, events invite a re-negotiation of conventional meanings and allow explorations of the boundaries of gender and sexualised codes.

In this overview of the research imbrications between gender and events, a discrepancy is to be noted. As already addressed in a previous section of this introduction, gendered experiences, politics and imaginaries are mainly investigated in events, which are shaped by gender-sensitive, equality-provoking ambitions. Due to the limited variety of events, research conclusions emphasise an emancipatory notion of gender and gender equality. With a lack of attention to celebrations, which are not predominantly aspiring transformation towards a more equal society, resources on conservative gender work in event settings are limited. Due to very few exceptions (Goulding and Saren, 2009; Johnson and Up Helly, 2019 Aa For Aa, 2019; Tokofsky, 1999; Ware, 2001), I return to this discrepancy in the final chapter of the book and suggest that further research of different types of events is required in order to understand the synergies between gender and events more holistically.

When the party meets its politics – making meaning in events

In discussing the socio-cultural significance of events and the entanglements of celebrations with the lived, politicised and imaginary potential of gender, this introduction establishes my point of departure. Events do not just serve a purpose of pleasure or commerce. Rather, conceptually framing the relationship between gender and events enables an understanding of celebrations as tools for meaning-making.

In the light of the developments of the contemporary festival industry, this process of meaning-making is under considerable dispute. As addressed in this section, the critiques regarding LGBT+ Pride events illustrate well the difficult dichotomy between meaning-making and impact-measuring. A growing number of activists and scholars tend to reduce the political influence of contemporary event industries to the commercialisation, institutionalisation and normalisation of their political contents.[15] For example, studying LGBT+ Pride events, Taylor (2014: 33) summarises the debate through the following provocation: "The question […] is whether pride has been reduced to festivalized spectacles of Otherness in the marketing of cities and commodities. Or is it still able to maintain its potential for political and sexual agitation?"

Informed by this questioning of the political potential of events, this book proposes a more nuanced understanding of celebrations. While celebratory events are mainly associated with factors of entertainment and consumerism, the reduction of events to a mere party would not do justice to their socio-cultural significance, as argued previously in reference to the multiple examples. I argue that – even in compromises – political negotiations are taking place in event settings. The challenge lies in the reading of festive events beyond a binary interpretation between party and politics. Kates (2003: 6) suggests that the boundaries of this duality need to be blurred because the "commercial, artistic and political arenas" overlap, interchange and mingle into a network, which cannot distinguish between party or politics. Rather, I consider festive events as "parties with politics", according to Browne's (2007: 63) suggestion. Kates (2003: 8) elucidates:

> In this way, meanings of […] festival[s] evolve over time, sometimes politically charged and rebellious, sometimes commercialized and 'corporate', but usually existing in a dialectic tension, reflecting the morass of social conditions and political agendas in which the festival itself is embedded.

The consideration of "parties with politics" (Browne, 2007: 63) grants space in order to acknowledge the evolution of festive events, their inherent contradictions and necessary compromises. The party as well as the politics require appropriate attention in order to balance the different stimuli in festive occasions.

Notes

1 Further addressed as UKCOC.
2 Further addressed as Hull2017.
3 Further addressed as COC.
4 Further addressed as ECOC.
5 Eventual restrictions of the term are addressed in a later section of this introduction and in the conclusion of the book.
6 See Bartie (2013), Black (2007), Brewster et al. (2009), Byrne (1987), Cohen (1980), Cohen (1998), Costa (2002), Gorokhov (2015), Leong (2001), Mccartney and Osti (2007), and Quinn (2003).
7 Similarly, as addressed in the clarification of the term 'gender' in the section above, I acknowledge that gender cannot be read as a singular notion when researching the socio-cultural significance of celebrations and their experiences. Various "axes of identity, such as class, gender, age, ethnicity and sexuality" (Markwell and Waitt, 2009: 147) become present, interact

and interfere throughout celebrations. Therefore, as highlighted in the previous section, an intersectional reading of the entanglements between gender and events in relation to other aspects of identity strongly imbricate and shape the further discussions.

8 See Ammaturo (2016), Ammaturo (2016), Browne (2007), Hahm et al. (2018), Johnston (2007), Jones (2010), Kates (2003), Kates and Belk (2001), Kenttamaa Squires (2017), Luongo (2002), Markwell (2002), Markwell and Waitt (2009), Morris (2005), Waitt and Gorman-Murray (2008), Waitt and Stapel (2011).

9 See Browne (2009), Cvetkovich and Wahng (2001), Eder et al. (1995).

10 See Goulding and Saren (2009), Johnson and Up Helly Aa For Aa (2019).

11 I explain the notion in further detail in the first analytical chapter, *Engagements through equality*.

12 Carniel (2015: 146) summarises: "The concept [of homonationalism] denotes how acceptance or tolerance of previously marginalised sexualities has become a criterion for legitimating national sovereignty in both domestic and global discourses".

13 See Browne (2007), Jones (2010), Kates (2003), Kenttamaa Squires (2017), Morris (2005), Pielichaty (2015), Tokofsky (1999), Ware (2001).

14 The concept of liminality is further explored in Chapter 3, *Engagements through equality*.

15 The movement associates with the notion of 'Gay Shame', 'Pink Washing' or 'Rain Capitalism' with strong activist networks in San Francisco, Brooklyn and London. See Bernstein Sycamore (2004), Halperin and Traub (2009), Love (2007).

2 Reprogramming transformative ambitions

Observations of shifting ambitions in City/Capital of Culture initiatives

Celebrating transformations

In the introduction, I highlighted events' practices of meaning-making, their inherent synergies with gender and necessary interpretations as parties with politics from a conceptual point of view. The interrogations in this chapter sit at the intersection between the previous conceptual elaboration and further explorations of the field. Next to dancing paper snippets of theoretical possibilities, bright, green letters guide my enquiry in this chapter.

The announcement, *Change Is Happening*,[1] is not just a statement sprayed on a back wall of an alley way; rather, it is an exclamation of

Figure 2.1 'Change Is Happening' at Humber Street/Fruit Market, 2016.

DOI: 10.4324/9781003121602-2

ambition and promise of perspectives. Using the city of Hull in the North of England and its celebration of the UKCOC title in 2017 as my analytical case study, I question the city's aspiration for transformation and explore how the socio-cultural value of gender equality is engrained in these celebrated ambitions for change. Therefore, I examine how Hull's "365 days of transformative culture" (Hull 2017 Ltd, 2015: 14) enable cultures of gender equality in the context of the event-led urban regenerative agenda.

Consequently, this chapter addresses COC initiatives in regard to their origins, structures and perspectives. Due to the framework developments, I discuss the initiatives' increasing emphasis on change. Informed by Immler and Sakkers' (2014: 23) observations of "(re) programming" trends, I examine the initiatives' heightened interest in cultural transformation. Also, as this chapter prepares for the further analytical debate of the empirical material, I include brief discussions on the field conditions and methodologies determining my ethnographic research.

City/Capital of Culture – origins, structures and interests

Established in 1983 and first celebrated in 1985, the ECOC initiative constitutes the origin of the global COC movement. The event format has had ripple effects as various initiatives in other geographical contexts followed the model (European Commission, 2009; Green, 2017). One of the latest spin-offs is the British interpretation of the national UKCOC award. While the ECOC and UKCOC initiatives differ in administrative and geographical parameters, their relations are omnipresent, which enables a connected conceptual and empirical discussion.

Since its inception, the purpose of the ECOC has been to celebrate the richness and diversity of Europe[2] through an exploration of common histories and shared connections. The initiative is grounded in the conviction that the political and geographical space of Europe shares cultural synergies. Former Greek Minister of Culture and ECOC initiator, Melina Mercouri argued that Europe cannot be understood solely as a political and economic space. In order to legitimise relations, she pointed out that Europe needs to be addressed as a cultural space equally (European Commission, 2009). Therefore, ECOC events intend to bring European residents closer together, as they provide "opportunities for Europeans to meet and discover the great cultural diversity of [the] continent [...]. The [ECOC] promote[s] mutual understanding and intercultural dialogue among citizens and increase[s] their sense of belonging to a community"

(European Commission, 2015: 1). According to this description, Sassatelli (2002, 2008, 2009) and Lähdesmäki (2011, 2013a, 2013b, 2014) emphasise that the ECOC initiative contributes as a symbol of European cultural policy to the construction of the entity of Europe and its identity.

The widely celebrated success of Glasgow and Liverpool as ECOC in 1990 and 2008 inspired the UKCOC award. The national Department for Culture, Media and Sports developed the UK-wide programme in consultation with the appropriate administrations in Scotland, Wales and Northern Ireland. Phil Redmond, initiator and chair of the independent advisory panel for the UKCOC initiative, outlines the title as an inspiration, ambition and ownership for the host city:

> [The UKCOC] is more than just a title. It is a focus, a rallying cry, a call to action, an opportunity to create and innovate, to build local pride, to show the world who you are and what you can do. It can inspire, instil a sense of ambition and provide the base for a real step change. And of course, it is a platform for a year-long celebration of local cultures and the great cultural diversity of the UK today.
>
> (Department for Culture Media and Sports, 2013: 3)

Redmond (2009: 2) considers the UKCOC programme to be a "badge of authority", as the host city becomes the centre of attention of the national cultural scene during its tenure. While each year two cities are designated as ECOC, the UKCOC title is awarded on a four-year-rota: Derry/Londonderry held the first UKCOC title in 2013, followed by Hull in 2017; Coventry is the third city to be awarded the title with its celebrations taking place in 2021.

Eventful transformations – City/Capital of Culture developments and trends

Throughout the past 35 years of COC initiatives,[3] executive models and trends have shaped the contemporary event frameworks.[4] On an operational level, time-scales and budgets have expanded drastically in current COC celebrations (Bianchini et al., 2013). While the initial awarded cities programmed a few weeks or months for the festivity, current COC hosts celebrate the title throughout the full year of designation. Furthermore, with a growing interest in the event's legacy, programming timeframes even look beyond the nominated year. Simultaneously, costs have increased immensely. This is not only linked to the extended timescale, but further influenced by the heightened competition and professionalisation of the initiatives, the executing sectors and the related ambitions (García and Cox, 2013, Cox, 2013).

Next to operational developments, changes in the initiatives' intentions are particularly important for the purpose of this book. Immler and Sakkers (2014: 4) summarise:

> Although the original idea of this cultural programme was to stimulate European awareness in order to support political unification, the [ECOC] title [...] has been used in recent years not so much to communicate Europe than to position a certain city as a cultural capital, to promote its international image and to solve local problems.

Regenerative ambitions strongly characterise COC initiatives. This attention to transformation derives from Glasgow's pioneering role as ECOC in 1990. While the first host cities were world-famous and well-known for their cultural, artistic and historical importance, Glasgow presented a very different profile. Harnessing its declining industrial image and successfully transforming the city's cultural assets through the COC celebration, Glasgow was the first city to use its tenure for urban regenerative purposes and therefore serves as a crucial point of reference in the development of the initiatives' intentions. Lille, ECOC in 2004, Liverpool, ECOC in 2008 and Essen for the Ruhr, ECOC in 2010, are more recent examples of celebrations with strong regenerative interests and widely recognised successes through hosting a COC event. In the context of the ECOC initiative, transformative aspirations developed seemingly organically.

Contrary to this linear storyline of progression towards event-based, culture-led regeneration in the COC initiative, the UKCOC programme addresses regeneration as a central driver in the national competition. In the document, *Guidelines for Bidding Cities*, the Department for Culture, Media and Sports (2013: 3) elucidates:

> The overall aim of the [UKCOC] programme is to encourage the use of culture and creativity as a catalyst for change. [...] Cities and areas that bid for the title will need to spell out [...] how they will use it in making a step change in their area and creating a lasting legacy.

While regenerative interests have developed throughout the history of the ECOCs, urban transformation is mentioned as a central aim of the UKCOC award. Consequently, COC initiatives have become synonymous with urban regeneration (European Commission, 2010, 2015).

Alongside the practical developments, scholars study the ambition for event-based regeneration through COC events with specific attention to the economic, social and cultural perspectives. Even though the discussions imbricate each other, I address these three dimensions separately in order to provide an overview and situate my own research in the context of the scholarly canons. With interest in economic profitability, the majority of scholars approach COC events as an important catalyst for urban regeneration due to the economic impact potentially achieved within the COC tenure. Thus, the economic research perspectives develop in three strains of debate. Firstly, with their study of Salamanca as ECOC in 2002, Herrero et al. (2006) exemplify discussions of the economic dimension, as they estimate the direct and indirect benefits and expenses of the event. Secondly, Campbell (2011) outlines important discussions regarding the profitability of cultural industries and their relevance for further investment. Critically opposed to the former considerations, a small number of academics raise a third point of debate, as they identify and criticise the commodification of arts and culture.[5] Entangled but not always clearly acknowledged within such parameters, research on tourism and COC events needs to be taken into consideration in relation to the economic regenerative impact.[6] Discussions concerning social regeneration through the event framework emerged in the early 2000s. Here, cultural participation and public perceptions are core issues of enquiry. Research interests are guided by the adaptations of the ECOC guidelines, which highlight community engagement as an objective of the event.[7] Several scholars, such as Fitzpatrick (2010) on Liverpool ECOC 2008, address the social dimension critically, as they question how power relations are constructed and affected through the celebration of the title. The cultural dimension of COC events is interpreted in two ways. On the one hand, research of this dimension stresses the development of cultural industries and infrastructures through the urban celebrations.[8] On the other hand, scholars address the socio-cultural values inherent in the production of COC events. Therefore, celebrations of transnational, national and regional identities are central concerns in research perspectives regarding the event framework.[9] Considering the ambitions for economic, social and cultural transformation, in my research, I concentrate on the cultural dimension of the aspired change and thus further explore the notion of 'culture' in the context of COC events.

Where is the culture in a city of culture?

As highlighted in the previous sections, COC initiatives started out as cultural projects with an interest in raising awareness of the commonalities and diversities in national and international contexts. However, as the initiatives progressed, cities' ambitions centred on the potential for urban regeneration. Quinn (2009: 249) claims that the ECOC "has lost sight of its original cultural aims and is being increasingly used to further city branding, image creation and tourism revenue generation agendas". While the regenerative potential of COC events is noteworthy, scholars are increasingly asking: where is the culture in a COC event?

Examining the response to this enquiry, Immler and Sakkers (2014: 3) observe a "slight shift" in COC events "from a competition-based marketing of local identity towards a more universal value discourse" (Immler and Sakkers, 2014: 23). The scholars address this development as a (re)programming trend in the worldwide COC movement. While city branding and image campaigns accompanied COC host cities' agendas over the past decades, contemporary and future host cities move back to the "original cultural aims" (Quinn, 2009: 249) of COC initiative – as ambitions and aspirations are (re)programmed and centred on cultural transformation.

Studies by Lähdesmäki (2011, 2013a, 2013b, 2014), Boland et al. (2016) as well as my own research (Grabher, 2019) contribute exemplary insights into these shifting perspectives. With reference to ECOC's such as Pécs2010, Tallinn2011 or Turku2011, Lähdesmäki (2013a, 2013b) queries the ideological, political and cultural considerations that underpin and drive the celebrations. The researcher studies the negotiations of national and European identities in the context of ECOC events. With focus on the notion of cultural diversity, Lähdesmäki (2011: 32) argues that negotiations of the socio-cultural values are essentially political, as "the rhetoric used in discussing culture and identities in the [ECOC] program, is in itself profoundly ideological". Another example of shifting research interests in regards to COC events is Boland et al.'s (2016) exploration of the curing effects of culture in the case study of Derry/Londonderry's celebrations of the UKCOC title in 2013. The scholars observe that peace processes and a "culture for the cure"-approach frame the celebration. Boland et al. (2016: 6) elucidate:

During the 70s–80s–90s, cultural antagonisms were the cause of the conflict, whereas in 2013 cultural expression was perceived as curative. [...] Given this, [Derry/Londonderry] represents an important case to critically examine culture as a [...] peace resource.

The authors highlight the relevance of the event for its curing potential in consideration of its negotiation of culture through artistic mediation.

In my PhD research, *Gendering Cities of Culture*, I used Lähdesmäki's (2011, 2013a, 2013b, 2014) and Boland et al.'s (2016) attention to the production of socio-cultural values in COC events for my interrogation of the case study of Donostia/San Sebastián as ECOC in 2016. With the slogan, *Culture of Co-existence*, the city's application for the title embraces the socio-cultural potential of COC events. Encouraging explorations of the ways in which humans live together in the specific context of Donostia/San Sebastián and the Basque Country, but also in the broader context of the European and global community of nations, the event contributes to a re-evaluation of the capacities of COC celebrations (Grabher, 2019). Lähdesmäki's (2013a, 2013b) research on Pécs2010, Tallinn2011 or Turku2011, Boland et al.'s (2016) consideration of Derry/Londonderry2013 and my own study of Donostia/San Sebastián2016 exemplify the negotiations of socio-cultural values in COC events. Hence, these approaches to event-based cultural transformation enabled me to investigate the productions of cultures of gender equality in the context of Hull2017.

The city in the centre – notes on the field

As outlined in the introductory section, *Rationale, aim and structure*, my investigation of the negotiation of cultures of gender equality concentrates on the single case study of Hull2017. With this focus, I respond to the European Commission's (2009) acclaimed success factor of COC initiatives as well as to the context-sensitivities of the production of socio-cultural values. In order to situate the empirical analysis in the following section, I discuss the city of Hull, the celebration of Hull2017 as well as the investigated activities within the year-long programme.

Hull, short for Kingston upon Hull, is situated at the junction of the Humber Estuary and the River Hull in the administrative region of Yorkshire and the Humber in the North of England. The city counted 259,778 inhabitants in the national estimation of 2019 (Office for National Statistics, 2019). Surrounded by smaller villages, which make up the East Riding of Yorkshire, the city forms the urban centre of the region. As a port city, its geography is orientated along the riverbanks and spreads into the hinterlands. The city is marked by an East, West and North separation, in which East and West are separated by the River Hull and the related industrial area. The three zones of East, West and North Hull show very different socio-economic and demographic profiles. The areas are further structured into neighbourhoods, which developed historically or were explicitly constructed in different urban developmental phases (Hull City Council, 2019). Residents' identifications with neighbourhoods in the East, West or North zones are marked through associated cultural and sportive assets.

The city was first mentioned in the twelfth century and named Kingston upon Hull under King Edward I in 1299. It gained importance in trade, due to the access to the North Sea provided by the Humber Estuary. Trade connected the city with Scandinavia, the Baltic region and the Low Countries. At their height in the eighteenth and nineteenth centuries the whaling and fishing industries influenced Hull's urban growth. The accumulated wealth and importance of the port city was the reason for major bombing during World War II, during which 95% of the city centre was destroyed or damaged. In the 1950s and 1960s, the city recovered from the war in economic and social terms. While Hull experienced another prosperous decade in trading and fishing, the 1970s saw a collapse of the city's industry due to the decline of the European fishing industry (Hull City Council, 2019). The town's population has dealt with the socio-economic consequences of this decline ever since. Hull was the third most deprived local authority out of the 326 local areas in England (Culture Place and Policy Institute, 2018). Such negative statistics and related descriptions mark the city's internal and external perceptions greatly.

As "a city coming out of the shadows" (Hull City Council, 2013: 4), in 2013 Hull was awarded the second UKCOC title for 2017. In competition with Dundee, Leicester and Swansea, the selection panel appreciated Hull's interest in and dedication to community engagement, the role of the private sector and focus on legacy. Embedding the bid in a long-term urban regeneration plan, rhetorics of transformation were deeply engrained in Hull's celebration of the UKCOC title. In 2014, Hull City Council set up the independent company and charitable trust Hull 2017 Ltd to deliver the event. Martin Green, former Head of Ceremonies at the London Olympic and Paralympic Games 2012, led the company as CEO and artistic director. He and his executive team were supported by a board of trustees chaired by journalist and cultural commentator Rosie Millard. The goal of Hull 2017 Ltd (2015: 14) was "to deliver 365 days of transformative culture through a range of diverse and high profile cultural events and projects". Through four seasons, namely *Made in Hull, Routes and Roots, Freedom* and *Tell the World*, the year included over 2,800 events, installations and exhibitions (Culture Place and Policy Institute, 2018).

The programme of cultural activities is one of the most visible features of a COC event. As a curatorial act, every single activity in a COC event contributes to its overarching vision and identity. Consequently, my investigative interest concerning the production of cultures of gender equality centred on the event schedule of the year-long celebration of Hull2017. For the purpose of my ethnographic research, I examined six cultural activities as a sample selection of Hull2017's programme. Through qualitative and quantitative content analysis of the bid book, programme booklets and further publications by Hull 2017 Ltd, I identified cultural activities with gender-sensitive profiles in their form, content and/or purpose. The selection of these equality-themed events was further fine-tuned in consideration of the timescale, location and artistic genre of the identified activities. The following outline schematically presents the selected activities including their format, timeframe and location.

As Table 2.1 indicates, multi-platform festivals or associative event formats dominated my selection of cultural activities. Additionally, I investigated two exhibitions. The activities related to a fixed schedule of relatively short duration and I intentionally chose events spread throughout the celebratory year. Within the year-long programme of Hull2017, gender equality was a key area for the celebration. Major festivals including the *Women of the World Festival*, the commemorative *LGBT50* celebrations and the annual *Freedom Festival* placed the city's transformative process in a gender-sensitive, equality-themed agenda. Due to the narrative line of this book, I integrate the presentation of each equality-themed event into the analytical chapters.

Table 2.1 Schematic outline of selected activities in Hull2017

Title	Format	Dates	Location
Women of the World Festival	Festival	10–12.3.17	Hull City Hall, various locations in the city centre
SKIN: Freud, Mueck and Tunick	Exhibition	22.4–13.8.17	Ferens Art Gallery
Assemble Fest	Festival	3.6.17	Various locations on Newland Avenue
LGBT50	Event Series	22–29.7.17	Various locations in the city centre
Freedom Festival	Festival	1–3.9.17	Various locations in the city centre
Hull, Portrait of a City	Exhibition	13.10–31.12.17	Humber Street Gallery

Ethnographic encounters with the urban spectacle – notes on methodology

Following the brief introduction of the field, I provide notes towards the methodological approach and research practices of this book in preparation for the further analytical chapters. Due to spatial restrictions, this methodological discussion serves only for introductory purposes.

In summary, the study anchors in an ethnographic research approach, which draws upon feminist methodological principles. The fieldwork and analysis developed inductively and I primarily work with qualitative research material. The field conditions allowed and required innovative approaches regarding the research methods. Therefore, while working with traditional ethnographic practices of interviewing and participative observation, I emphasise novel interpretations of the original techniques, which are informed and inspired by feminist principles of knowledge production.

This research is designed in relation to the triangulation of the politics, practices and perceptions of cultures of gender equality in Hull2017. I investigate the politics of gender equality through political actors, who curate the event's cultural programme. The practices are portrayed through cultural actors such as artists and producers, who engage artistically with cultures of gender equality. Furthermore, residents contribute to the perceptive interpretations of cultures of gender equality, as produced by the political and practical perspectives. I borrow this triad from a common understanding of the art market, which refers to the institution, artist and audience as key stakeholders in artistic productions, as Hlavajova (2017) summarises. While in the research design my focus was on the actors constituting my research field, in the process of analysis my attention moves away from the stakeholders towards the practices of gender equality.

Due to the explicit attention to power structures in research contexts, I situate myself in the methodological debate opposing positive ideals of value-free, truth-seeking objectivity. Drawing upon classical feminist literature by Haraway (1988), Harding (1987a, 1987b, 1993) and Mies (1983), I recognise the relevance of social values in research. Therefore, I employ the concept of 'strong objectivity', as developed and discussed by Harding (1987a, 1987b, 1993): in light of feminist approaches to knowledge production, Harding (1987a) encourages the development of a different interpretation of objectivity. She argues that all knowledge is socially located. Consequently, there is no value-free research, as no society or scientific community is free of hierarchical structures. Therefore, Hirsh et al. (1995: 202) suggest that "[m]aximising objectivity

Table 2.2 Political actors – pseudonym, professional role, affiliation

Pseudonym	Professional role	Affiliation
Coby	Production	HULL2017 Ltd
James	Management	HULL2017 Ltd
Sabrina	Management	HULL2017 Ltd

in social research requires not total value neutrality, but instead, a commitment by the research to certain values". Informed by this methodological approach, my ethnographic research practice combined participative observations with qualitative interview techniques.

I held semi-structured interviews with political and cultural actors, who in a professional capacity were involved with Hull2017. The categories 'political' and 'cultural' are specified by the actors' most immediate affiliation.[10] As the table below indicates, I interviewed three political actors who worked for Hull 2017 Ltd. The 18 research participants categorised as cultural actors professionally affiliated with one of the investigated events. Furthermore, as addressed through the rubric 'professional role', I generally differentiate political and cultural actors through the three roles of Artist, Production and Management (Grabher, 2019).

Furthermore, for the purposes of this book, I developed a collaboration with a team of so-called observing-participants – nine residents of Hull and the East Riding of Yorkshire – who visited, explored and observed selected events for the purpose of the research. The term 'observing-participant' is a deliberate word play in reference to the method of participative observation. Describing the team members as 'observing-participants' rather than 'research participants' highlights their active involvement and crucial contributions to the research process and analysis. This collaborative research practice uses an experimental, participative approach to qualitative, ethnographic research in event settings. Invited to join any event according to their availability and interest, observing-participants were asked to document their participation in events and other activities through fieldnotes, audio-visual material and social artefacts. After each event observation, I met up with participants individually for a follow-up conversation, to discuss the experiences and record their reflections. Additionally, I held two focus groups with the team at the end of the year-long collaboration. In my further analysis, I strongly draw upon data deriving from this fruitful research collaboration, as it provides powerful insights into the

Table 2.3 Cultural actors – pseudonym, professional role, affiliation

Pseudonym	Professional role	Affiliated event/institution
Abbie[11]	Production	Women of the World Festival
	Production	Assemble Fest
Alice	Artist	Assemble Fest
Arthur	Artist	Women of the World Festival
Bahar	Artist	Women of the World Festival
Claudia	Artist/ Production	Women of the World Festival
Erin	Production	Hull, Portrait of a City
Eva	Production	Freedom Festival
Harry	Artist	Assemble Fest
Henry	Production	LGBT50
Hugo	Artist	Hull, Portrait of a City
Jess	Artist	LGBT50
Laura	Artist/ Production	Freedom Festival
Lily	Production	Freedom Festival
Max	Artist/ Production	LGBT50
Mia	Production	SKIN: Freud, Mueck and Tunick
Oliver	Artist	Assemble Fest
Thomas	Artist	LGBT50
Tim	Artist	Freedom Festival

audience's perception of events. The selection of observing participants was based on purposeful sampling in respect to age and gender. The following table presents a summary of all observing participants, listed alphabetically by pseudonyms with indication of their age group and gender identification. Furthermore, I indicate the events which each participant visited (Grabher, 2018).

For the data analysis, I employed the method of qualitative content analysis. I use the strategy according to Mayring's (1991) technique of coding and categorisation. My data analysis was based on a semi-inductive approach. The three main codes of engagement, performance and infrastructures of equality were pre-scripted. While these clusters were already set, the strategy of qualitative content analysis allowed me to further generate codes and categories within as well as beyond the framework fairly loosely.

Table 2.4 Observing-participants – pseudonym, age, gender, event attendance

Pseudonym	Age	Gender	Visited activities
Alex	18–24	Male	• SKIN: Freud, Mueck and Tunick • LGBT50 • Hull, Portrait of a City
Anna	25–34	Female	• SKIN: Freud, Mueck and Tunick • Assemble Fest • LGBT50 • Freedom Festival • Hull, Portrait of a City
Daniel	25–34	Male	• Women of the World Festival • SKIN: Freud, Mueck and Tunick • Assemble Fest • LGBT50 • Freedom Festival • Hull, Portrait of a City
Emma	25–34	Female	• Women of the World Festival
John	35–44	Male	• Hull, Portrait of a City
Mathilda	25–34	Female	• SKIN: Freud, Mueck and Tunick • Assemble Fest • LGBT50 • Hull, Portrait of a City
Rachel	45–54	Female	• Women of the World Festival • Hull, Portrait of a City
Rosa	65–74	Female	• Women of the World Festival • SKIN: Freud, Mueck and Tunick • Assemble Fest • LGBT50 • Freedom Festival
Sophia	35–44	Trans-Female	• Women of the World Festival • SKIN: Freud, Mueck and Tunick • Assemble Fest • LGBT50 • Freedom Festival • Hull, Portrait of a City

Notes

1 The slogan *Change Is Happening* and its associated design is used by Hull-based developers Wykeland, who are leading the regeneration of the Marina District to establish it as a new urban quarter and the cultural hub of the city. The area was formerly the site of a large-scale fruit and vegetable

market, which became derelict in the 1990s and has been revitalised through the regeneration plans. These plans are not necessarily connected but rather coincided with the celebration of the UKCOC. The intertwined regenerative processes share and create a strong atmosphere of transformation in the city.

2 Referring only to countries within the European Economic Area.

3 In order to observe the developments and trends of COC initiatives, references are strongly guided by the original European programme owing to its longer history. However, considerations also apply to the UKCOC award, as celebrated in Hull in 2017.

4 The contemporary ECOC guidelines emerged through three administrative developments. Since 1999, the competition for the title depends on a national rota, in which each year two Member States of the European Union are designated to compete for the title. An international, independent panel is responsible for the selection of the host cities. In 2006, the European Commission introduced a monitoring process and the Melina Mercouri Prize. If the monitoring panel considers the preparations for hosting the title appropriate, the prize supports the awarded cities with €1.4m. In 2014, further developments were agreed upon. From 2021 onwards, the administrative progress introduces a new rotation system, in which every three years an international competition opens for cities outside EU boundaries. Through this extension, the European Commission offers countries with an interest in joining the European Union to present themselves via the initiative. See documents outlining the policy developments: The European Parliament and the Council of the European Union (2006, 2014).

5 See Fitzpatrick (2010), O'Callaghan and Linehan (2007), Tucker (2008).

6 See Åkerlund and Müller (2012), Falk and Hagsten (2017), Gehrels and Landen (2015), Hughes et al. (2003), Richards and Wilson (2006).

7 See Boland (2010), Boland et al. (2018), Dragićević et al. (2015), Fitjar et al. (2013), Giovanangeli (2015), Hudec and Džupka (2016), Hunter-Jones and Warnaby (2009), Moulaert et al. (2004). Ploner and Jones (2019), West and Scott-Samuel (2010).

8 See Bergsgard and Vassenden (2011), Campbell (2011), Cohen (2013), Griffiths (2006), Quinn (2009), Umney and Symon (2019).

9 See Aiello and Thurlow (2010), Bianchini and Tommarchi (2020), Boland et al. (2016), Bunnell (2008), Devlin (2016), Dragoman (2008), Immler and Sakkers (2014), Ingram (2010), Iordanova-Krasteva et al. (2010), Lähdesmäki (2011, 2013a, 2013b, 2014), O'Callaghan (2012), Patel (2013), Žilič-fišer and Erjavec (2017).

10 I need to declare that a strict differentiation between political and cultural actors is not always possible. Many political actors carry responsibilities of cultural production. At the same time, many cultural actors are influential in the management levels of their affiliated event or companies. The categorisation is based on their primary responsibilities.

11 Abbie was interviewed twice, as she produced *Women of the World Festival* as well as *Assemble Fest*.

3 Engagements through equality

Studying encounters and dynamics of audiences in equality-themed events

How change is happening

In Chapter 2, I referred to the slogan, *Change Is Happening* and introduced the transformative ambitions underlying Hull2017. I clarified how the event frameworks of COC celebrations imbricate with ambitions of urban regeneration and proposed that this transformative potential enables the negotiations of socio-cultural values. In the following three chapters, I discuss how these transformations are put into practice. As COC events allow change to happen, I explore how this change is taking place in relation to the investigated production of cultures of gender equality in the context of Hull2017.

The next three chapters respond to the analytical triangulation of research perspectives: according to the common understanding of the art market, I consider the audiences, performers/performances and institutions/infrastructures as key stakeholders in the transformative negotiation process (Hlavajova, 2017). In my investigative approach, this focus on the stakeholders' triad translates into three analytical thematic clusters of practices negotiating and producing cultures of gender equality. Thus, I regard how audiences engage, events perform and infrastructures condition the production of cultures of gender equality. This triangulation allows a differentiated account of how events put socio-cultural values into practice. Obviously, the three analytical clusters continuously overlap, merge and entangle. However, for investigative purposes, I separate the analytical theme into three chapters. In the first analytical chapter, I address the encounters and dynamics of engagement, which are expressed, experienced and arranged in the investigated events in Hull2017. In the second chapter of the analysis, I examine how cultures of gender equality are performed and therefore negotiated in the context of the researched activities. Finally, in the third analytical chapter, I discuss how infrastructures condition the

DOI: 10.4324/9781003121602-3

negotiation of cultures of gender equality in the researched equality-themed events. Consequently, I create a holistic view of three crucial domains that shape and enact the transformative potential of the event as outlined in Chapter 2.

Encounters of equality – exploring patterns of engagement in equality-themed events

Observing-participant Rosa inspires my thinking about audiences and their engagements with equality, as she explains:

> I mean, I think a lot of people [...] who turned up for anything will have taken some little thing. You can't help [it,] if there are things going on around you to pick up some pieces. But you have to go to the more targeted smaller events. There are in the street things of course, but you have to go to the smaller targeted events to really engage in a more significant way. (Rosa, Observing-Participant, Interview, August 2017)

With increasing pressure on audience development, engagement has become an essential element in the planning and management of events. However, as Rosa points out in her observation, engagements in events can take place in multiple ways. Her observation results from the week-long event series entitled *LGBT50*, which commemorated the 50th anniversary of the partial decriminalisation of homosexuality in England and Wales. Next to large-scale events such as the first ever *UK Pride Parade and Party*, local actors organised lectures, exhibitions and performances related to LGBT+ history, culture and politics. In her capacity as observing-participant, Rosa attended the parade, several lectures as well as other activities in the series. While eagerly participating in various events, she is aware that engagements are happening also by "people turning up and taking something with them" – even if it is just "some little things". Rosa leads me to understand that independently of whether participation takes place in continuous, immersive volunteering or through distant observations of a spectacle, any engagement creates an encounter and holds the potential to provoke reactions. On this basis, I take the notion of engagement further and consider even intentional disengagement as a form of participation (Matarasso, 2018).

Inspired by Rosa's considerations, the analysis of the production of cultures of gender equality in Hull2017 begins with a focus on audience engagement. Through the following analysis, I argue that the celebratory community, as well as each participating individual, is shaped by the events and their contents. Furthermore, the accounts, observations and reflections by research participants indicate that events are equally shaped by the communities and individuals visiting them. The analysis shows that in the experience-based setting of events, audiences are key contributors to celebrations. In the following sections, I explore how selected events allow interactions with equality to take place, before discussing several observed dynamics in the investigated celebrations.

Engaging with events – conceptual considerations

My interrogation of audience engagements with cultures of gender equality is based on a phenomenological understanding of events: according to Getz (2007), an event is an immediate, experience-based condition. These experiences occur spontaneously in the moment of their happening, which gives celebrations their assumed provocative, transformative potential. In order to conceptualise such experiential accounts of events, I draw upon the concept of liminality by Victor Turner (1969, 1974, 1982, 1987a, 1987b, 1989), as briefly addressed in the introductory chapter of this book.

Initially developed in relation to his study of rituals in the 1960s, liminal event experiences are characterised as a time out of time, in a place out of place with the potential to create norms out of the norm. The temporal and spatial features of the liminal experience are captured through the exceptional circumstances marked as distinct from the daily routines and time schedules. Furthermore, spatial alterations influence the experiential scope. Victor Turner (1987a: 76) explains:

> Truly [the festival] is the denizen of a place that is no place, and a time that is no time, even where that place is a city's main plaza and that time can be found on an ecclesiastical calendar. For the squares, avenues and streets of the city become, in [the festive occasion], the reverse of their daily selves.

Intrinsic to these temporal and spatial features of liminality, I further characterise event experiences through the potential of creating norms out of the norm. Victor Turner's (1969, 1974, 1982, 1987a, 1987b, 1989) concept of liminality is determined as the experience of the subversion of existent normative structures. He describes subversion simply as: "[…] in liminality people 'play' with the elements of the familiar and defamiliarize them" (V. Turner, 1974: 60). Therefore, in the liminal momentum, the social structures, norms and relationships are discontinued; social boundaries negotiated; eventual rights and obligations suspended. With respect to the circumstances of events, Abrahams (1987: 178) translates liminal experiences of festivals as follows:

> Festivals manufacture their own energies by upsetting things, creating a disturbance "for the fun of it". [...] Festivals work (at least in their inception) by apparently tearing the fabric to pieces, by displaying it upside-down, inside-out, wearing it as motley rags and tatters.

According to Abrahams (1987), event experiences are sensations of supposed disruption and destruction, in which power dynamics are re-evaluated.

With this characterisation enters my curiosity for the transformative capacities of liminal experiences. Do these destructive moments hold transformative potential? While liminality is a temporally and spatially limited concept and subversive atmospheres of event experiences pass, Victor Turner (1969, 1974, 1982, 1987a, 1987b, 1989) argues for the necessity and essence of these breaking points in strictly structured and stratified societies. He suggests that experiences of liminality leave traces within the normative conditions of society and even goes as far as to proclaim that society's desires and imaginations become visible within the liminal expressions of festive encounters. The festive subversion of the norm in events supplies societies with goals, aspirations and structural models, capturing transformative ambitions that celebrations entail. Therefore, liminal event experiences can challenge boundaries, allow explorations and enable experimentation free from traditional social constraints.

Obviously, this potential for transgression needs to be read within its own restrictions. While events in relation to their liminal experiences are celebrated – maybe even worshipped – for their subversive energies, discussions of the conceptual and practical limitations ground the hype. Due to the limited space here, I can only briefly sketch two elements of discussion. Firstly, I argue that subversion constitutes a privilege. As pointed out by Pielichaty (2015: 239), celebrations need to be understood in the juxtaposition "between celebratory chaos and a social vehicle employed to maintain order and discipline". While in liminal experiences, "individuals [...] momentarily lose themselves and behave in a care-free manner", this "chaos" is disciplined to be "limited, constrained and restrictive" (Pielichaty, 2015: 239). Hence, the question arises: who can afford to "lose themselves" and be "care-free" (Grabher, 2020)? The second restrictive aspect within the debate on liminal event experiences and their transformative potential results from the practical development of the event sector as a branch of industry. In the introductory chapter, I described the ongoing festivalisation trend and the connected increasing institutionalisation and professionalisation of the event sector (Newbold et al., 2015). Consequently, the liminal event experience and the above discussed potential for transgression needs to be read in light of the profit-orientated, commercialised turn of the festival industry (Grabher, 2019).

Time out of time, place out of place and norms out of the norm capture events and their related experiential accounts. With awareness of the restrictions through disciplining and commercialising tendencies, the subversive potential of event experiences provides fruitful grounds for the study of engagements in cultures of gender equality in the context of Hull2017.

Cheering for equality – audience interactions in equality-themed events

Taking these conceptual interpretations of event engagements as a lens for my empirical considerations, I focus the analysis on how audiences interact with equality in the selected events. Thus, my analytical attention is framed primarily by the notion of 'conversation', but I also pay attention to more subtle forms of interaction such as the meaning of applause.

Describing the intended event engagement, the term 'conversation' is particularly prominent in the *Women of the World Festival*. The three-day, multi-arts festival dedicated to issues of gender equality was held for the first time in Hull in 2017. While the festival brand originates from the South Bank Centre London and is franchised nationally as well as internationally, the local festival programme was strongly driven by the intention of "starting the conversation" (Abbie, Cultural Actor, Interview, March 2017), as Abbie, a member of the production team, explains. She highlights that festival environments generally allow people to gather; therefore, in the context of the *Women of the World Festival*, the festive encounter is intended to create a platform in which participants can meet and enter into debate. Motivated by her interest in "starting the conversation", I traced accounts of these conversational encounters taking place in the context of this equality-themed event.

Regarding the reflections by the team of observing-participants, I note that conversations as an interaction with equality are taking place on two levels. On the one hand, participants report personalised, intimate contacts with the subject matter. On the other hand, festivals are experienced as collective, shared opportunities of exchange.

Being exceptionally attentive to her own learning process in the course of various event engagements, observing-participant Anna reflects on how the various festival participations affect her personal growth:

> On a very basic level, it made me realise [...] how big [a] hunger I have for just [...] seeing something. It moves something in my head and just opens some new ways of thinking and some new reflections [...] and it is just making me realise that I don't have it that often here in Hull.
>
> (Anna, Observing-Participant, Interview, August 2017)

Even though her reflections are in relation to a different festival, her response perfectly describes how the personal conversation becomes an interaction with the theme of gender equality. In addition to Anna's account, I count multiple statements of residents who gather inspiration and affirmation through their participation in the selected activities: Emma's (Observing-Participant, Interview, March 2017) realisation that she "want[s] to change jobs" or Rachel's (Observing-Participant, Interview, March 2017) consideration that it is "ok to have lumps and bumps" are just two examples from the *Women of the World Festival*, which demonstrate how equality-themed events start a conversation by encouraging personal reflections. On the basis of these insights, I agree with the previously cited authors Markwell and Waitt (2013) that events are an invitation to visitors to question and re-think their personal positionalities and relations to gender equality as an interaction – a conversation with oneself – is taking place.

Alongside the personalised encounters with equality through event experiences, the dialogical meaning of conversations receives heightened attention as an effect of events engagement. Observing-participant Sophia experiences and appreciates the conversational opportunities created within the celebration of gender equality. She takes the observations of conversations a step further and relates the dialogical potential to the needs of the urban society. From her point of view, conversations are a way to construct and maintain networks contributing to and expanding the production of cultures of gender equality. In respect to the *Women of the World Festival*, she elucidates:

> Women came together at that event and will then potentially socialise more with each other, realise that there are issues that they are all

interested in and carry on their own sort of conversations about [...] those issues. [...] It might mean that the women in the city will shout a bit more; having had this platform once, they will say "right, we can have this platform again", and they will shout a bit more to have that.
(Sophia, Observing-Participant, Interview, March 2017)

While Anna experiences the engagement with equality-themed events as an encounter with herself, Sophia addresses the conversation as an encounter with a wider collective. Both accounts immediately reflect Abbie's previously expressed ambition to create conversations in and through the festival. As a consequence, celebrations appear to offer space and time to encounter oneself as well as the wider community within the context of cultures of gender equality.

Beyond mono- and dialogical conversational opportunities, I regard more subtle gestures and actions as encounters with equality in the investigated activities. Hereby, I pay attention to applause and cheering as a crucial interactive modality in festival settings. Scholarly debates and popular media engage with the history, cultural differences and rhythmic physics of applause. The anthropological significance is described as a sign of approval, gratitude and support (Berlins, 2007; Kluge, 2011; Mann et al., 2013; Voicescu, 2012). Without going into further depth concerning the academic conceptualisations of applause, I regard the expressive nature of this interaction and its contribution to the production of cultures of gender equality. In much more abstract ways than conversations, applause and cheering highlight a personal and collective formative process. In her first observation opportunity, observing-participant Sophia focuses on the act of clapping during the opening ceremony of the *Women of the World Festival*. She notes: "Every applause moment was for a woman. That [was] great" (Sophia, Observing-Participant, Interview, March 2017). Her observations relate to the presentation of the so-called *Hull Trailblazers*: women of Hull championed by the festival committee for their influence in campaigning for social justice and equality in the city. Sophia acknowledges that the recognition of these trailblazers by the festival committee was an important act of equality in itself. However, in an interactive, engaging way, the audience's applause served as a form of further approval, acknowledgement and support to the selection and celebration of these women and their work. This symbolic encounter becomes even more explicit, as Sophia sarcastically remarks: "It was interesting to see, which women got the most applause and which ones didn't" (Sophia, Observing-Participant, Interview, March 2017). The research partici-pant addresses applause and cheering as a crucial contribution to the celebrated value of gender equality. The sound of clapping hands and cheering crowds provides an opportunity for the individual and the collective to encounter cultures of gender equality and significantly shape the celebration of socio-cultural values.

Navigating inclusion and exclusion – audience dynamics in equality-themed events

From the analytical focus on encounters and interactions with equality, my attention shifts to the connected consideration of audience dynamics. Thus, I interrogate the collected material in order to understand strategies, practices and processes of engagement in equality-themed events. One key concept stands out from research participants' descriptions: equality-themed events embrace the coming together of a community. Reported as a sensation of togetherness by residents and discussed as a strategy of inclusion by political and cultural actors, this engagement dynamic characterises the event experience and the overall celebration of equality.

Empirical narratives concerning a communal feeling in equality-themed events strongly resonate with Victor Turner's (1989) conceptualisation of communitas. As a consequence of liminal experiences, the scholar observes a collective sense of communitas. While he initially developed the concept, Edith Turner's (2008, 2012) further discussion is more fruitful for the study of events. She describes the sensation of communitas as "a group's pleasure in sharing common experiences with one's fellow" (Turner, 2012: 5). Influenced by liminal sensations, communitas creates a magical and unique atmosphere of a festive context as individuals meet in a celebratory community. Edith Turner (2012: 3) writes: "[the collective experience] comes unexpectedly, like the wind, and it warms people toward their fellow human beings. It arises when people let go into negative capability, which itself is a condition of creativity, a readiness without preconceived ideas". Edith Turner (2012: 3) argues that in the pleasurable moment of the common experience, identities do not merge, they exist alongside each other, as "each and every person are alive to the fullest". In other words, communitas is characterised by loose ends. The oneness respects the individuality but creates collectivity and communality through the shared experience.

Sensations of togetherness

While I address the value of togetherness in the third chapter, *Performance, events and equality*, this section focuses on the sensation of togetherness as an audience dynamic that influences engagements with equality. The concept of communitas finds resonance on empirical grounds, as residents acknowledge, value and even emphasise the sensation of togetherness as a substantial dynamic moving the festive community. I could list a large number of statements from various observing-participants sharing experiences associated to the conceptualisation of communitas. However, to achieve analytical depth, I focus on observing-participant Mathilda's depictions of the sensation. Her statements stand out as she shows particular awareness of and fascination for the collective experience.

In her observations of *Assemble Fest*, Mathilda acknowledges a particular dynamic that she sees engrained in the festival. *Assemble Fest* is a theatre festival in a high street in one of the neighbourhoods of the city of Hull. The ethos of the festival, as expressed in the slogan *Performances, where you least expect them*, affects its dynamics immensely, as shops, bars and street corners on the high street become stages for theatre performances of 20–30 minutes. As a site-specific event, the one-day festival does not take over the street but merges within the pre-existing infrastructure in playful ways. Audience dynamics are therefore crucial to the atmosphere of the festival not only in Mathilda's observations, but in the general set up. She summarises the relevance of togetherness in the context of *Assemble Fest* as follows:

> [The Festival] brought people out of their houses and away from the smartphone [...] to actually come and see what people can do first-hand and I think that was bringing people together. All of these City of Culture things [are] doing that. Just to see the streets full of people – young, old, whatever – just seeing everybody out en masse was magical. I like it a lot.
>
> (Mathilda, Observing-Participant, Interview, June 2017)

Her particular attention to the collective sensation crystallises in an activity as part of *Assemble Fest*. The musical walk-about, *The Chase*, connected members of the festival community by inviting them to parade along with musicians and performers. This performance served Mathilda as an example to illustrate her experience of the festival in particular and celebrations within Hull2017 in general. She explains:

> The community added on bit by bit, so it was kind of an accumulative feeling. Everybody was just coming together in this mass that was stopping the traffic with help from that [human dressed like a] zebra crossing the road. [...] I liked it a lot. I really enjoyed it.

I don't know, I don't know what word I am looking for. [Long Pause] It made me feel good.

(Mathilda, Observing-Participant, Interview, June 2017)

The musical performance, which brings people together so even the traffic has to stop, serves as a strong image and illustrates metaphorically the dynamics of togetherness, which Mathilda observes and enjoys. In a later observation of *LGBT50* and particularly the *UK Pride Parade and Party*, Mathilda returns to her powerful observations regarding the sensation of togetherness. With an undertone of annoyance, as she felt she was repeating the same observations in regard to various festivals and celebrations, she elucidates:

I think I said it a million and one times: it is everybody coming together. [...] This is a weird thing about the [celebratory] community. So, it is a community bringing everybody together, celebrating their individualness – their individual identities, their individual preferences or whatever. So, it is a bit of a weird one, it is unity but at the same time diversity.

(Mathilda, Observing-Participant, Interview, August 2017)

Everybody joining in unity with an attention to each other's particularities is an essential element for Mathilda's experiential take on the coming-together in an equality-themed celebration. Similarly to Edith Turner's (2008, 2012) outline of the concept of communitas, the unified mass has its peculiarities, individualities and uniqueness within. The collective and communal are a strongly knit sensation, but simultaneously open for personal expressions and impressions. Even employing similar words to Edith Turner (2008, 2012), Mathilda observes communitas as a sensation of togetherness in the unique, magical atmosphere of equality-themed events.

Echo chambers

Mathilda's enjoyment of togetherness is contested by other observing-participants. Questioning who can participate in this coming-together of a community, residents point out so-called "echo chambers" (Daniel, Observing-Participant, Interview, March 2017) as a reoccurring audience dynamic in equality-themed events. In order to illustrate this descriptor, observing-participant Daniel refers to a performance and its usage of humour in the *Women of the World Festival*: while the punchline is narrated, laughter is returned from the audience. In this moment,

Daniel considers that the narrative and response work like an echo. Dependent on the particular audience members and their expectations, reactions are already pre-written. Therefore, according to Daniel, sensations of togetherness necessarily become echo chambers, in which audiences are "accomplice[s] of the narrative" (Daniel, Observing-Participant, Interview, March 2017). The participant is particularly aware of this dynamic in the context of the *Women of the World Festival* and explains further:

> I think it is like reinforcing an idea, which we all agree upon already. [...] Yes, an echo chamber [...]. Because we are already agreeing in the entrance. We don't need [the cultural actors] to tell us about [gender equality]. Therefore, I am telling you it is like we see a club, where we all already belong.[1]
>
> (Daniel, Observing-Participant, Interview, March 2017)

As a result, equality-themed events are observed to speak only to the accomplices.

Reflecting upon these eventual echo chambers of equality, Abbie, a member of the production team for the *Women of the World Festival*, argues that one of the difficulties of equality-themed events is the assumed target audiences of the celebration. She explains:

> The issue we always had creating a festival called *Women of the World* was that 'women'. It looked like we were just focusing on women. Even when we tried to combat that, we [...] met with so much resistance, because it is 'women'. So, it is just for women like "Oh, it is not for me, it is for women". I remember inviting my dad [...] and [he was like,] "it was just for you women". and I was like, "No, that is not the point". But [...] it is still that issue.
>
> (Abbie, Cultural Actor, Interview, March 2017)

Abbie's explanation is crucial to understanding the expectations that are attached to the production of cultures of gender equality. The notions of equality construct a symbolic barrier regarding thematic accessibility. Even though this was resisted and worked against by political and cultural actors, there tends to be an invisible boundary created by the assumptions and interpretations of the thematic focus on equality.

While I recognise the critiques and risks of echo chambers, I also need to highlight their beneficial implications regarding professional and personal development. Alice, a member of a local feminist theatre company, explains that the company's thematic focus on gender equality is a niche within the theatre sector in the city and region. This niche creates a "marketing question", as their thematic focus generates a community of "followers", who "enjoy seeing that [kind] of work" (Alice, Cultural Actor, Interview, October 2017). The dynamics of an echo chamber is profitable to their work, as the company can count on more or less stable audience numbers. Alongside Alice's professional considerations, observing-participant Sophia highlights the positive contributions of echo chambers for her personal experience of equality-themed events. Referring to the *Women of the World Festival*, Sophia considers her particular seating position between groups of men during the opening ceremony. Being surrounded by men, she explains that she felt alienated from her expected club of female accomplices. She remarks that the encounters with like-minded people – particularly women – over topics of gender equality was an important motivation for her festival attendance (Sophia, Observing-Participant, Interview, March 2017). While equality-driven echo chambers can be critiqued for their exclusionary tendencies, the audience dynamic contributes to a sensation of collective encounters with equality. Consequently, Daniel acknowledges: "It is this club of friends, this echo chamber; but still, there are always things to discover or remember or refresh" (Daniel, Observing-Participant, Interview, March 2017).

Strategies of inclusion

The experiences of togetherness (and eventual echo chambers) require a strategic reading: the audience dynamic is not only occurring organically but is strongly influenced by the interests of political and cultural actors. Inclusion serves here as the keyword that characterises the aspiration of event producers and directors of Hull2017. Similarly to Finkel et al.'s (2018: 2) observations, "inclusion is a ubiquitous term" in this research. Thinking carefully about the usage of this terminology, the strategies of inclusion refer to the notion as a way for "people to participate in society as it is constructed" (Finkel et al., 2018: 2). Generally described as a coming together of the community, inclusive strategies are enacted in a variety of ways, but inclusion is central to the dynamics of equality-themed events.

The theatre festival *Assemble Fest* serves as an important example for highlighting this strategic perspective. Abbie, a member of the production team for *Assemble Fest*, explains her motivations, strategies and practices of inclusion as follows:

> [I kept] thinking about what are the barriers that people experience going to theatre and I think *Assemble Fest* has been very much

about not only supporting artists, but breaking down those barriers and that is part of the way we are doing it on a high street. So, it is literally on people's doorsteps. We do it in businesses, where people would usually go but also where they wouldn't go. So, there is a beautiful kind of thing in encouraging people to try out and see amazing spaces that they don't go into. [We are] trying to create this live experience and that live thing of going into a space and seeing it and hoping people go back.

(Abbie, Cultural Actor, Interview, June 2017)

Abbie further explains that accessibility frames the interest of inclusion for the festival. The UKCOC event employs a similar approach, as James, a senior manager of Hull 2017 Ltd, explains:

I think the bigg[est] drivers were the inclusion driver. [...] We wanted to make sure that the programme worked right across the city both by doing and producing work within communities and within geographies. But also, if we were doing work in the city centre by hopefully ensuring that it was open and accessible [to] whoever wanted to come to it. So, possibly the answer [to the question of the values of Hull2017] is that our focus was a demographic and geographic approach [to inclusion].

(James, Political Actor, Interview, December 2017)

On the micro scale of a one-day festival as well as on the macro structure of the year-long event, inclusion serves as a crucial interest, in order to support the audiences and encourage their engagements. Inclusive strategies in the context of *Assemble Fest* and the project of Hull2017 foster accessibility for potential audiences. Through reduced barriers and increased accessibility, visitors' curiosity is piqued, which potentially leads to the engagement of new audiences.

Limitations to inclusion

In discussion of the notion of inclusion, research participants draw my focus to the limitations of the strategies and their related implementations. The critique is driven by a concern for whom or what inclusion applies. Observing-participant Anna's experiences guide me in the formulations of the limitations of inclusion in Hull2017. While sharing multiple inclusive, diverse and welcoming experiences, she encountered strategies of exclusion in relation to her activism against the financial partnerships of Hull 2017 Ltd. Throughout 2017, a small group of residents mobilised against the sponsorship of Hull2017 by the oil company British Petroleum.[2] Joining a national campaign, the activist group raised critiques concerning the art-washing of the brand to distract from the company's environmental and human rights violations. The Hull-based activist group continuously intervened in a year-long lecture series, explicitly sponsored by BP. The activists' provocations took the form of asking a question in the Q&A after each lecture. Anna's experience of intervening challenges the reach of inclusion of Hull2017. In a focus group interview, she explains:

> It's not part of the [...] events that we have been to for the research, but I have been [...] to these [lectures] at the University and I asked a question concerning the BP sponsorship, which the people on the stage didn't like. [...] [In my question, I pointed out the contradiction of] City of Culture [...] being sponsored by BP [...] [when] Hull is in danger [of] being flooded as an effect of global warming. [...] So, they didn't reply to it. [...] So, yes, I wasn't welcomed with the question. They didn't want to answer the question and actually this moment made me feel like [...] it is not including all aspects of me and of people around me. So, [it seems that] if we have any sort of critique, we are just being silenced.
>
> (Anna, Observing-Participant, Focus Group Interview, November 2017)

In her description, Anna downplays the organisers' and audiences' reactions. In an informal conversation, she told me that organisers tried to physically stop her intervention by demanding the microphone from her while she was still speaking. Additionally, attending several lectures myself, I experienced the audiences' reactions and noted they became harsher each time the question was asked – moaning, booing as well as yelling were recorded. Anna reflects on these physical and symbolic barriers as practices of exclusion. Regarding the analysis of inclusion as an audience dynamic, I agree with Anna's personal conclusion that certain critiques and critics "are just being silenced".

Engagements of transformative potential?

In respect to the encounters with and dynamics of equality-themed events, research participants' reflections show how cultures of gender equality are explored through the celebratory setting.

Underlying the engagements with equality, the collected narratives address the transformative potential of event experiences. While personal and communal transformations are frequently reported, research participants continuously debate the depth of the event-based potential for transformation. In the citation introducing this chapter, which I reproduce here, observing-participant Rosa points towards the varied intensities of encounters in the celebration of equality. As previously addressed, she explains:

> You can't help if there are things going on around you to pick up some pieces. But you have to go to the more targeted smaller events. There are in the street things of course but you have to go to the smaller targeted events to really engage in a more significant way.
> (Rosa, Observing-Participant, Interview, August 2017)

Beyond the various forms of engagement, which I referred to at the beginning of this chapter, Rosa's judgement further questions the potential for engagements with equality in relation to the aspired cultural transformation.

Reviewing the empirical material, I observe a stark contrast between cultural actors' intentions and residents' perceptions of the transformative potential of celebrations. The desire, aspiration and necessity for transformation is omnipresent in the contrasting considerations of cultural actors and residents. Artists and producers identify transformative encounters as a key interest and motivation for their work. For example, Abbie, a member of the production team of the *Women of the World Festival*, declares: "What I wanted to do particularly with [this] festival was to offer an opportunity for everybody. [The festival serves] as a way [for] people to engage with the ideas, the debates, some of the issues that are out there" (Abbie, Cultural Actor, Interview, March 2017). While the desire for engagement with gender equality is acknowledged by residents, they critically question the efficiency of these intended encounters in order to create change. In their critique, the notion of 'change' correlates with a demand for effectiveness. Observing-participant Alex synthesises:

> I think like in that sense [engagements with equality through celebrations] are not effective. I don't see it as an effective form of social change, but like that is my damning critique of the whole thing. [...] It didn't change.
> (Alex, Observing-Participant, Interview, August 2017)

Alex's doubt is reaffirmed by observing-participant Daniel's remark concerning the idiosyncrasies upon which the celebration of equality build:

Nowadays, protesting is no longer standing in the front line. Nowadays, protesting is dancing in the city like in gay pride. Nowadays, it turns out that protesting for the rights of homosexuals – or whoever – means you participate in a stupid concert, in a park with a beer.[3]

(Daniel, Observing-Participant, Interview, September 2017)

The observations of Alex and Daniel empirically illustrate my previous conceptual discussions of the restrictions of subversive event experiences. While cultural actors share their commitment to transformation in the form of event-based encounters with cultures of gender equality, observing-participants criticise the assumption of societal change. Beyond sharing his observations, Alex raises suggestions and particularly pays attention to the temporal restrictions and the need for continuity:

I feel like again and again: [...] where is the space for continued conversation? [...] [I] just feel like we haven't succeeded over the whole year in fostering [...] critical conversations. I don't feel that we have succeeded even beginning to get some conversation[s] off the ground. [...] Especially in terms of [...] an increasingly divided society, where these kind of conversations [...] need to happen. [...] This isn't creating genuine conversations.

(Alex, Observing-Participant, Interview, October 2017)

While acknowledging that encounters with equality do occur within festival spaces, Alex points out that the continuation of encounters is essential to the transformative potential of event engagements.

Notes

1 Statement translated by author from Spanish.
2 Further addressed as BP.
3 Statement translated by author from Spanish.

4 Performance, events and equality

Examining the production of cultures of gender equality in the performed contents of events

As the show goes on

According to the triangulation of the analytical perspectives, I move from the focus on audiences and their engagements to the performance of artistic contents in equality-themed events. Hereby, I investigate how cultures of gender equality are performed in the six selected activities from Hull2017.

In this analytical theme, I use the notions 'performer' and 'performance' as generic terms. These terms serve as the most encompassing notions in the complex arena of festival industries. Therefore, I address, among others, actors, moderators, painters and curators as performers. Exhibitions, parades, concerts and other cultural activities are performances. Rather than referring to a specific art genre, the notions serve as descriptors of all artistic practices and practitioners contributing to the programme of cultural activities.

The following analysis of performers and performances of equality emphasises the multiple influences that contribute to the production of cultures of gender equality in Hull2017. Rather than speaking of a singular story embraced by the year-long event, my analysis showcases multiple stories of equality. Incorporating various accounts of research participants, differing, diverging and even contradicting interpretations of equality and its celebrations become prevalent. Consequently, I synthesise that cultures of gender equality need to be considered as a reflective practice and shared responsibility, which embrace a plurality of meanings produced in the context of the investigated equality-themed events. This chapter demonstrates that the production of cultures of gender equality is not a solid entity, rather the opposite: fragilities of the notion and its practices characterise the performance of gender equality in the context of Hull2017.

DOI: 10.4324/9781003121602-4

The following chapter pursues two thematic lines. After a reminder of the conceptual framework underlying the analysis, I, firstly, explore what stories of equality are being told and interrogate how these stories unfold in the context of the investigated celebrations. Secondly, the analysis concentrates on the positionalities of performers of equality. Thus, I argue that the performers themselves become representatives of the celebrated values; they carry responsibility for producing cultures of gender equality.

Selling ideas – theoretical translations

This analytical chapter builds on the conceptual discussions addressed in the introduction to this book. Hereby, I pointed out that events are a political practice in particular cultural and social circumstances and therefore are negotiating values and creating meaning. Considering the enactment of gender and gender equality in events, I explained that the party and politics imbricate in celebrations (Browne, 2007). Consequently, I declared celebrations as platforms where socio-cultural values are being negotiated. My argument is informed by scholars such as Benedict (1983), Falassi (1987a) and Finkel (2015), who highlight the socio-cultural significance of events and their meaning-making practices. Falassi's (1987a: 2) consideration of celebrations as a "series of overt values that the community recognises as essential to its ideology and worldview". Benedict's (1983: 2) understanding of events as a way of "selling ideas" translate into my interpretations of events' capacities to construct meaning. Expanding on these processes of meaning-making in celebrations, Finkel (2015) further points out that events do not take place in a vacuum but are expressive of their zeitgeist. Therefore, the constructed meanings need to be read as situated in the socio-political and -cultural contexts. As previously cited, Baker's (2015, 2017, 2019) work on the *Eurovision Song Contest* illustrates how meanings of gender equality are constructed in the context of an event. Reflecting on the situatedness of the music contest, Baker (2017) observes that the event's developments correspond to general European discourses on gender equality. The scholar even goes as far as to declare that the event informs and works towards a European identity. Hence, the *Eurovision Song Contest* exemplifies how the socio-cultural significance of events can be understood. Regarding other examples such as the *Michigan Womyn's Music Festival* (Browne, 2009, 2011; Eder et al., 1995; Kendall, 2006) or the *Wild Ginger Witch Camp* (Jones, 2010), I showcased that processes of meaning-making are taking place on a personal, political and imaginary level. In accordance with Browne (2007), I suggested events create meaning, which expands societal imaginaries and challenges the status quo. The following interrogations of performers and performances in events derive from an understanding of the relevance of celebrations for the negotiation of socio-cultural values. On the basis of these conceptual considerations, my analysis of the production of cultures of gender equality highlights the constructions of meanings on the stages, walls and pavements marking festive encounters in Hull2017.

Stories of equality – visibility, empowerment and awareness

Independently, if identified as "quality" (Mia, Cultural Actor, Interview, August 2017), "value" (Abbie, Cultural Actor, Interview, June 2017) or "message" (Harry, Cultural Actor, Interview, June 2017), investigated artistic contents communicate stories. As lead artist of a community dance project affiliated with the *LGBT50* celebrations, Thomas relates communication as a core focus of his artistic practice and explains its relevance as follows:

> I see my art [as] a way of communication. Like a writer or an author would communicate what they are doing through words, I try to communicate it through theatre and movement. Whenever I create a piece of work, I try to rely on a subject matter to be educational, so you teach somebody something on some sort of level. I am not a choreographer that just works without structure or pure movement. I am not interested in that. I think movement can be a strong tool to portray [...] messages and ideas and ideologies and I think that is where the politics is. [...] Doing a movement is political, is saying something. So, I use my art as a tool to speak, to say, to communicate.
>
> (Thomas, Cultural Actor, Interview, July 2017)

In his choreography, Thomas declares movement as a form of expression and uses dance to tell stories of equality. His artistic practice serves as a medium through which to channel his voice. While I encounter performances that shy away from explicitly communicating qualities, values or messages, the majority of the investigated performances share strong interests in shaping narratives of equality.

Researching the *Women of the World Festival*, *Assemble Fest*, the *LGBT50* celebrations, *Freedom Festival* as well as the two exhibitions, *SKIN: Freud, Mueck and Tunick* and *Hull, Portrait of a City*, as part of Hull2017, multiple stories of equality emerge. Consequently, I do not claim to provide a comprehensive analysis of all potential stories.

Rather, I refer to a selection of the most prominent narratives of equality. For further clarity, I address the plurality of stories through a focus on the *LGBT50* celebrations, which took place in July 2017. As previously explained, the week-long event series included a variety of performances, including parades, concerts and exhibitions. While my explanation concentrates on this particular celebration, the three storylines co-exist in all examined events and therefore define Hull2017's stories of equality. I initiate the discussion with a focus on the representation of marginalised voices. Later, I introduce the notion of awareness as a story of equality. I finish by considering equality as a narrative of empowerment.

The first storyline highlights representation as a crucial theme for the celebration of equality. As a member of the production team of Hull 2017 Ltd, Coby highlights that in the *LGBT50* event series, the visibility of "minorities" (Coby, Cultural Actor, Interview, October 2017) is a key storyline. He explains:

> For me personally, the way I apply some of those values [of equality to the event] is through the idea of minorities. I hate using that term. But in a sense, [I refer with this term to] people, who feel isolated in the normativised conversations that cities have about themselves: what it is to be Hullisian? Or what it is to be the other? Good or bad? [The event seeks for those] minorities [to] feel that they have an ownership and citizenship in their city and they have an ownership and a right in the public. They have a right to express themselves freely in that space.
>
> (Coby, Cultural Actor, Interview, October 2017)

Coby explicitly relates to the representation of LGBT+ communities in the city and associates their visibility with the story of equality in the *LGBT50* event. The celebration and recognition – in further consequence: representation and visibility – of the LGBT+ community serves as a clear storyline for the festival. Coby's considerations of representation and visibility of minorities in equality-themed events resonates with Browne's (2007) observations of LGBT+ Pride events. Browne (2007: 66) points out that the "presence of sexual otherness [during Pride events] in otherwise heterosexualized urbanities" enables a temporal visibility for individuals and groups that could be considered, in Coby's terms, as minorities. The claim for visibility and representation in festivities like Hull's equality-themed events correlates with Ammaturo's (2016) observations, in which he points out that these celebrations enable temporal alterations of normative spaces with the potential for socio-cultural creation beyond the status quo. Conceptually, as well as empirically, the representation and visibility of minorities dominate the narratives of equality as celebrated in Hull2017. Even though some residents questioned whether minorities' visibility is key to the production of equality, their representation continues to be a highly demanded factor in the performance of cultures of gender equality.

The second storyline of equality in Hull2017 embraces the notion of awareness. Conceptually connected to the narrative of visibility but discussed separately due to its continuous presence in the empirical material, I observe a strong presence of awareness-raising campaigns in the celebration of equality in Hull2017. The awareness of the struggles for equality is particularly present in the context of the commemorative celebrations of *LGBT50*. This interest becomes clear in the reflections of Jess and Max who, in their role as artists and producers in the *LGBT50* event series, highlight the need to raise awareness of past, present and future equality concerns for the LGBT+ community. Working as the lead artist in a community craft project related to *LGBT50, Jess characterises this as a key element in his artistic practice*. He explains:

> It is telling stories; making those stories apparent; making people aware of them and [...] showing what has happened to make people understand that this is part of you, part of your history and it is still going on and it is really, it is really: how lucky people are now really.
> (Jess, Cultural Actor, Interview, July 2017)

On the one hand, as Jess describes, his artistic work is intended to make apparent and share the knowledge about stories of equality. On the other hand, in his final sentence, he highlights the importance of this awareness, in order to locate current situations within their contemporary and historical contexts. Alongside the artist's consideration, several members of the production team express similar interests in relation to the celebration of equality. As a member of a charity involved in the production of the event series, Max elucidates:

> I think [*LGBT50*] is about sadness and celebration. I think, it is about remembering what has gone on and what has to go on in the future. I think for many in 1967 it wasn't just that: right, we are alright now. 27th of July 1967[1] did not mean from that point on everything was fine. But, actually, it was the beginning of a change, an opportunity and empowerment for communities and individuals to get together.
> (Max, Cultural Actor, Interview, August 2017)

Max sketches the intention of the event and its consequent story of equality as a process of raising awareness. He argues that knowing about the past and present struggles of equality is important in order to understand current situations. The commemorative ethos of the *LGBT50* celebrations influences the storyline of the event and emphasises the awareness of the past struggle, current circumstances and future perspectives of equality.

As a final and crucial storyline, empowerment stands out as a buzz-word and omnipresent narrative in the investigated equality-themed events. Beyond statements of performers and producers, observing-participants frequently reflect on this storyline. I address the narrative of empowerment through the interpretations of the observing-participants Mathilda and Sophia. As members of Hull's LGBT+ community and highly active participants in the *LGBT50* celebrations, the two research participants agreed strongly on the empowering sensations that they experienced in the event series. Sophia's participation in a community dance project crystallises how stories of empowerment are written. Reflecting upon her experience, she points out that taking part in the project was an act of "showing no fear" (Sophia, Observing-Participant, Interview, August 2017). Deriving from a spoken word piece written for the dance performance, the phrase summarises her personal interpret-ation of the project as well as the general commemorative celebrations. She elucidates:

> "We are here, we are queer, and we are showing no fear." That message ran through the whole of the performance and the whole of the project. Showing no fear in terms of being visible, in terms of being out in the public. Showing no fear working with people from all different sides of the community. Showing no fear with something very big [...]. Showing no fear in committing. Showing no fear in committing parts of yourself to something emotionally. It was all about getting rid of fear, I think.
> (Sophia, Observing-Participant, Interview, August 2017)

Sophia explains that her experiences of "getting rid of fear" set the core story of the project. "Showing no fear" becomes an emblem of the empowerment discourse, which I continuously encounter in the research field. Expanding on Sophia's account, observing-participant Mathilda reflects upon empowerment as a story of equality in regard to her participation in the *UK Pride Parade*. She explains:

> "I am, who I am." [...] I lost track of how many times we sang that song during the weekend [...]. So, [it was saying] take me as I am or

don't take me at all. I think the self-acceptance and [...] individuality is the theme, I think: [...] "I am born this way." These are reasonably cheesy songs or like pride songs. [...] I don't know if they have deep meanings – but they all have a same overarching theme don't they: this is who I am, I am not going to change, because you might want me to or because you feel more comfortable about it and, yeah, let's just get on with our life really. That is the theme! That is the theme of these events, I always thought.

(Mathilda, Observing-Participant, Interview, August 2017)

While referring to "cheesy" song lyrics, Mathilda pinpoints their core message as an essential story of the event series: The celebration of equality empowers individuals and communities to be who they seek to be. Consequently, song lyrics, such as *I Am Who I Am* and *Born this Way,* frame a central quality, value and message of the commemorative celebration as they tell a crucial story of empowerment.

Entertainment and comfort – narrative strategies in Hull2017

In the previous overview, I emphasised what stories of equality are told in the celebration of Hull2017. Below, I explore how these stories are narrated. As outlined in Chapter 2, the selection of researched events includes multiple formats including festivals and exhibitions. The settings and contexts of these particular events guide the narrative strategies. However, I encounter two general narrative tactics common to all investigated equality-themed events. The two perspectives need to be read in relationship to each other but, for analytical purposes, are presented separately. In the first narrative strategy, I address entertainment. Secondly, I consider the narrative strategy of comfort as an approach to the celebration of equality.

Entertaining cultures of gender equality

Events carry an expectation of entertainment. Key words such as 'festival', 'fest' or 'party', are anticipated – or even required – to be fun. Observing-participant Rosa explains:

When people see the word 'festival', they expect to be entertained as well as informed – with the emphasis on the entertainment. In other words: a celebration, not a conference. Not that conferences are not celebrations. They are, you know! (laughing) But they are more serious. They are like more serious celebrations.

(Rosa, Observing-Participant, Interview, March 2017)

As suggested by the observing-participant, entertaining narrative strategies are inscribed in the celebratory contexts – maybe even embedded in the structure of an event (E. Turner, 2008, 2012; Turner, 1969, 1974, 1982, 1987a, 1987b, 1989). Therefore, entertainment is the first narrative strategy in the investigated celebration of equality.

In the programming process for the *Women of the World Festival*, the relationship between the narrative strategy of entertainment and the event's structure becomes apparent. As a member of the production team, Abbie synthesises the structural relevance of fun:

> [The *Women of the World Festival*] is very much an art-form festival, so it is about different ways of exploring these issues of equality without being a conference – without it being too intellectual.
>
> [...]
> [The programming] is literally kind of going: why aren't there more darts clothes for women? So, we had a darts pop up moment. How do we engage with trail blazers? They are coming in cartoons.
>
> [...]
> We flipped [around]: from a panel discussion to hula-hooping or a singing demonstration or a dance demonstration or a Bollywood demonstration. So that there were ways of getting people to realise that city hall isn't just a sit on your bum and listen kind of [space].
> (Abbie, Cultural Actor, Interview, March 2017)

The provision of fun elements appears to be central to the *Women of the World Festival*. As Abbie points out, alternative presentation modalities are crucial to the celebrations' capacities to produce cultures of gender equality. Therefore, entertainment is engrained in the communication strategy of the event.

I locate the source of this desire for entertainment in assumptions concerning audience engagements. Oliver, director of a local theatre company performing in *Assemble Fest*, addresses the company's interest in and usage of entertainment, as follows:

> I think [...] a lot of people make theatre to make a point a lot of the time, which is great and that is what theatre should do. But I think our starting point is that we want to entertain people. Then, through that you can start and feed in little bits of what you are trying to say. Because at the end of the day, if you don't entertain people, people are not going to listen. [...] It is about stories, it is about drama, it is about creating attention, and all of these things.

We like to make people laugh, because we like to laugh. So, we would like to make the stuff that we would like to laugh at.

(Oliver, Cultural Actor, Interview, June 2017)

The theatre director implies that entertainment is a tool for seeking attention, engaging the audiences and communicating messages. Therefore, beyond Rosa's and Abbie's considerations of entertainment as a structural feature of events, Oliver highlights entertainment and fun to be a crucial strategy for his artistic practice and the intended telling of the stories of equality.

Comforting cultures of gender equality

The second strategy, "comfort" (Anna, Observing-Participant, Interview, July 2017), interacts with the entertaining narrative line of equality-themed events. Strategies of comfort expand the previous discussion of entertainment as a communication tool in the celebration of equality. However, strong critiques by observing-participants of being made too comfortable require me to discuss this narrative line separately.

Observing-participant Anna introduces these reflections on the narrative strategy of comfort. Reflecting upon her participation in various performances in the *LGBT50* event series, she points out that the contents of the celebration felt easy and simple:

[The value of equality in *LGBT50*] is quite appealing and [...] quite easy. You know, being packed in colourful rainbow packages and just being sold to everybody around and people easily refer to it, easily find themselves in that. So, yeah, like spreading some kind of tolerance behaviours and also this consciousness of the whole history of it and knowledge about it.

(Anna, Observing-Participant, Interview, July 2017)

Anna's observation highlights a communication strategy that foregrounds the comfort of the audiences. As a member of the production team of the *Women of the World Festival*, Abbie reasons this approach by pointing out:

I mean one of the things that turns me off about the issues [concerning equality] is, when I meet people who are overly political about that. Because I cannot identify with that. I admire the passion, but it is not in my language and I think, if we want to really make change, then it has to be really accessible to everybody.

So, it is about how we find different ways of talking about it, so it is accessible.

(Abbie, Cultural Actor, Interview, March 2017)

According to Abbie, the communication strategy of comfort is connected to inclusive engagement interests, as addressed in the previous chapter. Abbie suggests that in order to make cultures of gender equality accessible, comfort plays a crucial role in the communication of artistic content.

Abbie's reasoning that comfort is an accessible strategy for fostering inclusion in equality-themed events provokes strong reactions from observing-participants. Oppositional to the cultural actor's claim, research participants perceived the narrative line as rather negative and even highlighted its patronising and harmful effects. Anna synthesises:

[Hull2017] until now, they are making you quite comfortable, rather than uncomfortable. It would be nice to make you uncomfortable. [This is] what art can be about. Not just making you feel like: "oh, you are so great. You are just so tolerant. You are just […] great. […] Lets just make a mental jerk-off all together [about] how great we are". But I think [maybe it is necessary too] sometimes to think that we are shit in some stuff. Maybe we have a long way still to go and just to be critical, be a little bit sad about stuff. [Maybe sometimes] try to be moved to some different attitude, rather than just this glad, comfortable self-indulgence.

(Anna, Observing-Participant, Interview, July 2017)

Anna's considerations respond to my conceptual critique of the liminal potential of subversion as a controlled momentum of chaos, as addressed in Chapter 2, *Engagements through equality*. In accordance with Pielichaty (2015), I question who is served by engaging with the "liminal space to momentarily lose themselves and behave in a care-free manner" (Pielichaty, 2015: 239). The alternated, subverted structures, norms and conventions are explored with the knowledge and security of returning to routine. Therefore, Anna's observations and critique of comforting effects feed into these limitations of the subversive potentials of events. Highly disturbed by comforting sensations, observing-participant Daniel demonstrates that the narrative strategy of comfort primarily serves the hegemonic communities of society. He refers to the simplicity and further regards the dangers that the mediated comfort provokes. His reflections derive from various activities he visited as part of *Freedom Festival*. The annual outdoor street festival takes place on the first weekend in September. The thematic roots of the event lie in the commemoration of Hull's famous resident William Wilberforce and his campaign for the abolition of slavery. The festival's creative team expands this commemorative purpose and addresses contemporary questions of freedom and human rights through artistic practices. Due to the scale, diversity and quality of the programme, *Freedom Festival* attracts local as well as regional visitors and is one of the biggest festivals in the city. Daniel is an enthusiastic visitor to the festival and joins several days of the event. Among other activities, he follows the crowd to watch a highly advertised community dance performance. The show, *Rush*, is "inspired by the post-2008 global cultural phenomenon of protest and riot, where all over the world people are showing their dissatisfaction with prevailing social and economic conditions" (Freedom Festival Trust, 2019). With strong interest in the theme, Daniel expresses his annoyance with the comforting sensations that he experiences as an audience member. He explains:

> It is very easy to do a show with, I don't know, 200,000 pounds and all the people in Hull say: "Together, we can"! It is saying: if you want to, you can. But people are losing their houses or are trapped in alcoholism. There was a statement [in the show] that said: "I don't want benefits, I want employment." This message is very strong. It is not a nice message. It is not a good message. [...] It is a message of mediocrity.[2]
>
> (Daniel, Observing-Participant, Interview, September 2017)

Rather than tackling the epistemic problem of injustice and inequality in their simplified expression and artistic beautification, comforting communication strategies dilute the actual topic that the artistic content aims to address.

Why are they there? Performers of equality

In my introductory discussion of gender and events, I do not provide an explicit theoretical approach to analysing the role of performers in events. From a Critical Event Studies perspective, cultural actors do not receive great conceptual attention. However, performers and their roles and responsibilities are referred to in the majority of interviews: when questioned about how performances of equality were perceived, research participants immediately responded to the inquiry with a reference to the performers of the investigated events. Therefore, while in my theoretical outline on the imbrications between gender and events I did not explicitly address performers and their role in events, the empirical material urges me to pay further attention to this element and its contribution to the production of cultures of gender equality in Hull2017.

Research participants' suggestions that the individual performers act as representatives for the celebrated values of equality spark my interest for this analytical theme. Observing-participant Sophia illustrates this relationship between the performers and the performances of equality in her reflections on the exhibition: *SKIN: Freud, Mueck and Tunick.* The "blockbuster exhibition" (Mia, Cultural Actor, Interview, August 2017) addresses the subject of nudity in the fine arts with a focus on the works of Ron Mueck, Lucien Freud and Spencer Tunick. Artworks from the permanent collection of the gallery further contribute to the exhibition's theme. During her visit, Sophia notices a gender imbalance regarding the artists on display. With the exception of Francesca Woodman, all exhibiting artists are male. Sophia reflects upon this lack of gender diversity and its effects, as follows:

> Ok, so, in terms of the artists' work on show, it is not very equal. [The exhibition] is about the body and how we see ourselves. But it is only from the male artist's point of view – almost exclusively.
> (Sophia, Observing-Participant, Interview, April 2017)

Sophia's observation of the exclusively male perspective on the theme of nudity leads her to point out the relevance of the performers' situatedness in the production of cultures of gender equality. She suggests that the performers' positionalities stand in direct correlation with the produced contents. Therefore, the performers are responsible for and become representatives of the presented performance and celebrated value of equality, which is further discussed in the following sections.

Representatives of equality

Inspired by Sophia's reflections concerning the role of performers of equality, I, firstly, examine how performers act as representatives to the celebrated cause of equality. Research participants highlight three different approaches to representation relevant to equality-themed events, which I summarise as the diversity strategy, tokenism pitfall and 'one-of-us'-approach (Rachel, Observing-Participant, Interview, March 2017).

Diversity on display

Observing-participants Daniel and Sophia summarise the diverse representative spectrum. According to their interpretations, diversity serves as a strategy which categorically interprets the identities of performers. Among others, gender, ethnicity, sexual orientation and age are key components in this representative approach. In the context of *LGBT50*, Sophia participates in a community writing project and notes the representative strategy to correspond to the following ethos: "They wanted a mix of voices. They wanted people from all different sectors of the LGBT+ community" (Sophia, Observing-Participant, Interview, August 2017). Similarly, Daniel acknowledges the representation of women in the *Women of the World Festival*. In retrospect, Sophia sees the diversity approach as an opportunity to give "a voice" (Sophia, Observing-Participant, Interview, August 2017), while Daniel points out that this diverse representative spectrum "is a statement. That is a declaration of principles" (Daniel, Observing-Participant, Interview, March 2017). Hence, both observing-participants take note of the performers and their diverse spectrum and further appreciate the message that this representative approach communicates.

Beyond the observing-participants' considerations, political and cultural actors eagerly voice their opinions and practices of diverse representations. When questioned about the production of cultures of gender equality, James, a senior manager of Hull2017 Ltd, and Henry, a member of an artists' collective involved with the production of *LGBT50*, agree on the relevance of diversity as a representative strategy in their curatorial approach to events. James elucidates:

> I think [diverse representative strategies] start in making sure that you have a balanced team. Because if you are going to believe in the curatorial act [of diversity] [...] then you have to have a team that reflects that. So, you know, we have a balanced team of people, so, therefore, different points of view would come in. People would point out that it was all getting a bit male and pale over there. I think it is a structural point from the beginning: [...] Unless you have a team that reflects the world you live in, you are not going to produce a programme that reflects the world you live in. So, you have to be very, very careful when you are hiring and creating a team that you have those differences in it. Well, it is like you never finish that.
> (James, Political Actor, Interview, December 2017)

In his explanation, James acknowledges the necessity for diversity, as he argues that a diverse team of performers strategically contributes to the aspired cultures of gender equality. Extending James' argument, I turn to Henry, who is acutely aware and critical of his organisation's practices. Henry agrees with James' consideration that the team's profile relates to the capacities for diverse representation. However, while James is generally convinced of the success of his diversity strategy and only briefly acknowledges eventual difficulties, Henry emphasises the challenges associated with diversity as a representative spectrum. He explains:

> We struggle. We struggle not to be male dominated. I think, even though we are a queer company, we are gay men. We are gay and we are queer. But we are still men and will still have that background. I am still a man, I still have all that kind of privilege or upbringing. [...] It is a big [issue] and I do think it is slightly unresolved – even in a queer company.
>
> (Henry, Cultural Actor, Interview, July 2017)

James and Henry's reflections consider and foreground diversity as a representative strategy crucial to the project of Hull2017. As a "declaration of principles" or a way "to give voice", cultural and political actors employ diversity as a strategy in their curatorial process and practice. With the awareness that it is a challenge to achieve a diverse representation, the cited research participants communicate awareness of the relevance and necessity of diversity.

Equality as a tick box exercise

While the diverse representation of performers is a clear focus in discussions of the production of cultures of gender equality, research participants are cautious of the misuse of these diverse strategies and call out tokenistic approaches in several investigated activities. While appreciating diversity as an appropriate approach, observing-participant Sophia notices that, rather than foregrounding diverse representation, some events were "ticking boxes" (Sophia, Observing-Participants, Interview, March 2017). In her observations of the *Women of the World Festival*, Sophia highlights: "They had some classical standards: [...] I felt that there was like [a] token black woman, the sexy PR friendly classical violin girls, and that sort of nod to Bollywood. It was conceived as ticking boxes" (Sophia, Observing-Participants, Interview, March 2017). The attention to representing marginal identities works as a tool for diversity mainstreaming; however, on several occasions, Sophia observes that sincere diversity strategies turned into a "tick box exercise" (Sophia, Observing-Participants, Interview, March 2017). She claims that strategies and tools of diverse representation become a mere calculation of visible or expressed identity categories with the expectation that equality is therefore achieved. However, according to her, strategies of diversity imply a level of reflexivity relevant to the production of cultures of gender equality.

While experienced and often judged by observing-participants, cultural actors' understandings of tokenism are particularly insightful. Henry, a member of an artists' collective involved in the production of *LGBT50*, verbalises the tensions underlying the discussion. Highlighting the need to showcase different voices, he expresses a reflexivity and awareness of diversity in his own event productions. He explains: "I mean the event itself will be driven and led by a queer female lesbian voice. So, she is at the front of the thing. She is the leader of the event" (Henry, Cultural Actor, Interview, July 2017). He shows great awareness of the relevance of diversity in his attention to the role of the "female lesbian" performer, while simultaneously acknowledging that some practices of diversity lead to a tactic of politicking and are vulnerable to tokenism. In order to distinguish between diversity strategies and tick box exercises, Henry raises a crucial question:

Who is it for? [Who is it for] when you are putting a drag on stage or a band or a fat bloke in a bath or a drag queen on a revolt or two guys doing dancing or a female drag queen or [...] a black queer activist talking about what it is like to grow up black and gay and masculine?

(Henry, Cultural Actor, Interview, July 2017)

Henry's provocative question, "Who is it for?", serves as a guide to navigate representative practices between the contrasting strategies of diversity and tokenism.

"One-of-us"-approach

Alongside observations of representative strategies of diversity and tokenism, observing-participants strongly support performers who are "one of us" (Rachel, Observing-Participant, Interview, March 2017). Extracted from Rachel's reflections of the *Women of the World Festival*, I understand the "one-of-us"-approach as an identification of the audiences with the performers' trajectories. Rachel illustrates the approach in relation to her enjoyment of meeting Karen Briggs, a celebrated world Judo champion born in the east of Hull, at the event:

"I knew that [Karen] was a Judo champion, but it was really interesting, because she was what I consider working class, like people I know. […] Karen's story from being working class to being a champion: that was good" (Rachel, Observing-Participant, Interview, March 2017). Observing-participant Rosa introduces a similar interest in or even expectation of nuanced selections of performers as representatives of equality. She explains:

> I think the festival was to show that [the performers] were ordinary women. They were not born with any particular advantages, but yet throughout their lives they looked for ways to express what kind of talents they had and eventually became successful. It was a good idea.
>
> (Rosa, Observing-Participant, Interview, March 2017)

Relating to what Rachel addressed as the performer being "one of us", Rosa refers to the representative potential of "ordinary women". Contrary to the strategies of representative diversity, identity markers are not the main focus; rather, the approach refers to the geographic origin or social class of the performer but could be expanded to various other categories of identification such as gender, sexual identity or ethnicity.

Responsibility for equality

The second analytical perspective regarding the performers' contribution to the production of cultures of gender equality focuses on their responsibilities for the produced content. Reflecting upon the line-up for the *UK Pride* concert, observing-participant Daniel triggers my analytical interest:

> Why are those artists there? Because they are gay? Is it because they are kind of like a flagship music for gay people? […] Maybe some were gay, maybe some wrote one song that says: "I will survive". […] It makes you wonder: Why are they there?[3]
>
> (Daniel, Observing-Participant, Interview, August 2017)

While Daniel does not seek an answer to his query, his provocative question, "Why are they there?", encourages me to understand performers' motivations and negotiation of this responsibility for equality.

Personal, political and professional motivation

In the collected interviews with cultural actors, I trace performers' motivations based on their personal, political and professional relationships with cultures of gender equality. Abbie, a member of the production team for the *Women of the World Festival*, frames this analytical focus: she introduces the relationship between personal positionalities and political convictions in her reflections on her professional engagement with the festival. Abbie explains:

> It is an interesting one for me because there were times particularly with this festival where I think there was an expectation that you have to be a feminist to engage with those issues or create those platforms.
> [...]
> When I took on the job, I was a little bit anxious slash hesitant, because I don't feel like I am a feminist.
> [...]
> We had various conversations about introduction statements and that they should be more political and I am not that person. So, it was quite good to go: "no, actually that is ok". It is ok, you know, being the programmer for the [*Women of the World*] festival without being an ardent feminist. Though, I am sure that there are some ardent feminist[s], who will probably come after me.
> (Abbie, Cultural Actor, Interview, March 2017)

In this statement, Abbie shares her concerns about programming an equality-themed event with me, as her personal interests somewhat contradict her political aspirations. In the first analytical encounter with this statement, I caught myself formulating a judgement about the lack of feminist interest and the implications for the programming of the event. However, after further analytical reflection, my attention shifts, as I become aware of the dependencies of the personal, political and professional motivations in regard to the performers' involvement in the celebration of equality.

Inspired by Abbie's honest statement, I trace similar relationships in the analysis of performers' motivations for their engagements with cultures of gender equality. The interplay between the personal, political and professional becomes most explicit in conversations with performers associated with the *LGBT50* celebrations. Dominated by white, gay, male performers, my question concerning the reasons for their dedication to gender equality was promptly met with the declaration: "I am a gay man" (Thomas, Cultural Actor, Interview, July 2017). On multiple occasions, I requested further reflections upon the relationship between the identification as a gay man and the professional commitment to issues of gender equality. Several performers clarify their understanding of this identity marker and outline how professional engagement and political awareness are written into their personal biographies. Jess, lead artist for a community craft project in association with *LGBT50*, explains:

> Gay politics is [...] something that attracts me deeply and defines who I am. This is a struggle that I still have in my life and I guess [my work] is a way of [...] working through [...] those politics. I still have problems with my parents and I am 60 and my dad is 91. My mom is 85 and they have known that I am gay for many years and they struggle.
>
> (Jess, Cultural Actor, Interview, July 2017)

In his statement, Jess reports how political struggles of equality are engrained in his personal biography. Hence, he addresses already in what way his artistic practices are relevant to professionally engage with personal and political realities. Thomas, lead artist in a community dance project affiliated with *LGBT50*, further elaborates and clearly relates the personal experiences of sexual discrimination with his creative work. He explains:

> I am a gay man. I am an openly gay man and I don't mind giving myself that label. But I grew up [...] in a very narrow-minded small village in Yorkshire, where being gay wasn't an option and it was a miners' village. It was dominated by white straight men with very traditional values and as a young gay artist, I wouldn't say it was hard, but there was definitely an oppression there. So, [...] I think by the time I got to my late teenage years, when I discovered my creativity, I used that as a tool to express my sexuality.
>
> (Thomas, Cultural Actor, Interview, July 2017)

Both reflections refer to biographical experiences as a source for the professional dedication to the production of cultures of gender equality. Similarly to Jess and Thomas, many performers highlight that their artistic practices are a way to work through personal issues as well as societal discriminations caused by the experience of gender and sexual oppression. Throughout all of my interviews with cultural actors, a pattern reoccurs, which associates the professional motivations of performers with their personal trajectories and political visions.

Negotiating responsibilities

Beyond the personal, political and professional imbrications constituting the motivations for performers' involvement with the production of cultures of gender equality, Daniel's provocation, "Why are they there?", also challenges how performers negotiate their responsibilities for equality. In our conversation, Max, a member of a charity involved in the production of the *LGBT50* celebrations, introduces his dedication as a duty of care. Reflecting onto the audiences and their experiences of the celebration of equality, Max clarifies the relevance of his work for the members of Hull's LGBT+ community:

> I think [...] [events are] engaging and valuable and so important for life, because when you are there and you are having a good time, it frees your mind up and I think that is the power of Pride. It does allow you to kind of think about things that perhaps are going on.
>
> (Max, Cultural Actor, Interview, August 2017)

With awareness of the origins of the event, the LGBT+ community and the linked struggle, Max negotiates his responsibilities as a form of care work. He carries such duty for equality with pride and caution, as he understands its value and fragility. Max's perception of his responsibility for equality is shared by Henry, a member of an artists' collective involved with the production of *LGBT50*. Henry points out that the responsibility for equality is given through the work with equality-themed subjects and genres. Beyond a cautious care for the subject matter, he is aware that his work has a wider responsibility for the political project of equality. However, he notes that in his work he enjoys the liberty to envision, shape and produce cultures of gender equality. Henry elucidates:

> It is our job to associate and engineer [...] a cultural product [of equality]. Yes, we are in the business of creating cultural products. We are making stuff up and [...] it is our responsibility from our heart [that] we want to socially engineer a better society.
>
> (Henry, Cultural Actor, Interview, July 2017)

The cultural actor considers himself a social engineer, whose product is equality. This dedication entails responsibility, as the vision carries a duty for the equal and just society he aspires to create. Max's understanding of care as well as Henry's approach to socially engineering the political project of equality strongly correspond to the conceptual considerations of the imaginary. As addressed in the introductory chapter in accordance with Browne's (2007) outline, next to the personal and political effects of events to the understanding of gender and gender equality, celebrations hold the capacity to shape societal imaginaries. As an act of care in creating a better society, performers' negotiations of their responsibilities for equality reproduce an understanding of the imaginary potential of celebrations.

Shared responsibilities

Alongside Max's and Henry's negotiations of responsibilities, Bahar introduces another valuable argument regarding the performers' responsibility for equality. In respect to my question about her understanding of her role in the production of cultures of gender equality, she points out that this responsibility needs to be conceived as a shared task. Commissioned as lead artist in a community craft project, Bahar contributes to the *Women of the World Festival*. She expresses gratitude for the opportunity to support the event's aspirations for equality. Nevertheless, Bahar is critical of the agendas that equality-themed events might attend to. She elaborates:

> It is all about the people who do the commissioning of the work: Is [the production of cultures of gender equality] really their agenda? [...] It is all about what is the real agenda of the person commissioning the work.
>
> (Bahar, Cultural Actor, Interview, March 2017)

According to Bahar, the production of cultures of gender equality relies on the performers and their performances. However, as she points out, these responsibilities are shared. The greater political context and its consequential structures influence the performers' capacities. While aware of her responsibility as an artist, she calls for more attention to the awareness of political actors in their function as decision-makers. Bahar suggests that the structural layers, in which performers operate, essentially determine the performer's capacities in the production of cultures of gender equality.

I take Bahar's observations as an invitation to address the polit-ical agenda with a key decision-maker of Hull2017. In discussion with James, a senior manager of Hull2017 Ltd, the duty, dedication and even obligation to equality take shape:

> [Working towards equality] is just something that you do, you know. And I feel very strongly, you need to gather a group of people, who would find it very odd to do anything else. (Laughing) It is a bit like the diversity argument, you know. You create work that reflects the world you live in and everybody lives in the world that I live in and we live in. So why would you possibly not create a programme that did that. You become mindful of it as you go forward.
>
> (James, Political Actor, Interview, December 2017)

James conceptualises his interest in and devotion to the production of cultures of gender equality. While I discuss consequential practical implications in the following chapter, *Equality in structure*, I appreciate and acknowledge his reflections and awareness of the duty of care, which Max initially describes.

Notes

1 On 27 July 1967, the UK Parliament agreed on the Sexual Offences Act 1967, which decriminalised same-sex intercourse between two male adults in pri-vate spaces (Hull 2017 Ltd, 2017).
2 Statement translated by author from Spanish.
3 Statement translated by author from Spanish.

5 Equality in structure

Investigating infrastructural conditions and the production of cultures of gender equality

Structural disputes

Bahar's considerations of the shared responsibility for cultures of gender equality bridge the previous and following analytical chapters. In her contribution to the *Women of the World Festival*, the artist clarifies that the responsibility for cultures of gender equality does not lie solely in the hands of the performers and their performances. Rather, she emphasises that equality is a collective project, which all levels of event production contribute to. While Bahar considers the explicit collaborative processes between cultural and political actors, observing-participant Alex considers closer attention to the "deeper structural level[s]" (Alex, Observing-Participant, Focus Group, November 2017) to be an analytical necessity. He explains:

> Maybe these equality things are going on. [Maybe] people's lives are getting transformed and that is amazing. But on a deeper structural level, I don't think it's facilitating and moving towards equality or it doesn't feel like it to me. It is like another [...] distraction away from [what actually needs to be changed in order to achieve equality].
>
> (Alex, Observing-Participant, Focus Group, November 2017)

In the second chapter, *Engagements through equality*, I touched upon Alex's doubt concerning the transformative effects of Hull2017: the observing-participant points out that he misses the "space for continued conversation" (Alex, Observing-Participant, Interview, March 2017) within Hull2017. Questioning the infrastructural conditions of Hull2017 and its production of cultures of gender equality, Alex's concern becomes more encompassing as he critiques not only a short-sighted understanding of change, but also addresses a serious lack of

DOI: 10.4324/9781003121602-5

structural transformation. While he acknowledges that "maybe people's lives are getting transformed" through engagements in equality-themed events, he raises concerns about how structures of inequality have been reproduced through the celebration of Hull2017.

Inspired by Bahar's and Alex's comments, this final analytical chapter interrogates the relationships between infrastructural conditions of Hull2017, the investigated events and the celebrated content of equality. I argue that infrastructural conditions are fundamental to the production of cultures of gender equality, as I outline how the event-based meaning-making processes are affected by infrastructural conditions and contexts. Concentrating on three dominant themes, the festivalisation of equality, the material conditions of events and the commercial tensions of celebrations, I concretise that the conditions of celebrations create a spectrum in which the aspirations for equality can be supported but simultaneously harmed.

The following chapter begins with the acknowledgement of a research gap. While the mainstream canons of Event Studies address operational and managerial concerns in events, festivals and celebrations, Critical Event Studies lacks a phenomenological reading of these infrastructural conditions. Consequently, the further analysis highlights not only how infrastructures condition the production of cultures of gender equality, but also showcases how event infrastructures can be investigated from a Critical Event Studies perspective. I outline in this reading of structural influences three selected issues addressed as the festivalisation, materialisation and commodification of equality in events. Differently than in the analysis of the audience engagements with and the produced contents of equality, the empirical results of this chapter are rather disenchanting. Inappropriate infrastructures have been frequently observed and commented upon by research participants. Therefore, I end the chapter with the question, So What?, and clarify that the political potential of events is not doomed due to the infrastructural conditions of events; rather, event infrastructures require further attention in order to support the imbrications between gender and events.

Conceptual gaps regarding infrastructural conditions of event-based production of socio-cultural values

In the conceptual discussion introducing this book, I paid little attention to the infrastructural conditions of events, festivals and celebrations.[1] Approaching events through a phenomenological lens, I deliberately distance myself from hegemonic debates in Event Studies. While the mainstream disciplinary canons engage strongly with the operational and managerial – addressed here as infrastructural – processes of celebrations, this investigative focus is not suitable to my interpretative framework of events. Informed and inspired by emerging discussions in Critical Event Studies, my conceptual framing of the relationship between gender and events highlights the socio-cultural significance of celebrations and their meaning-making potential, as I regard the influence of events in respect to the personal, political and imaginary realm of gender. Therefore, I argue that hegemonic debates on event infrastructures and operationality do not serve my investigative interest or purpose. However, the lack of phenomenological interpretations of event infrastructures leads me to slippery theoretical grounds. Even though, my conceptual outline does not allow a meta-discussion of the empirical accounts, the infrastructural conditions of events still are a key component in my empirical exploration of cultures of gender equality within Hull2017. I could shy away from this analytical angle; however, as I value the opinions, experiences and reflections of research participants, I engage with this crucial theme in acknowledgement of the theoretical limitations. Hence, in what follows, I ask how event infrastructures influence, condition and shape the celebration of equality. Hereby, I showcase how and why a phenomenological reading of these operational, managerial conditions of celebrations is relevant for the further production of cultures of gender equality.

Celebrating equality – observations regarding an ongoing festivalisation trend

Initiating the discussion of infrastructural conditions and their influences on the meaning-making potentials of celebrations, I, firstly, focus on the event-based production of cultures of gender equality. Thus, I question how the ongoing festivalisation trend, which Hull2017 embraces, affects the production of cultures of gender equality.

The notion 'festivalisation' can be understood in two ways. On the one hand, as used in the introductory chapter of this book, festivalisation describes the growing prominence of festivals in contemporary European urbanities. As mentioned in the introductory chapter, Newbold et al. (2015) and Cudny (2016) summarise that in the late twentieth century events have been increasingly used to effect transformative ambitions of urban plazas and streets among other venues. In accordance with Cudny (2016), the concept of festivalisation influences my general understanding of the research field of COC events and their urban regenerative potential. On the other hand, I employ the notion of festivalisation in order to describe my observations of the programming strategies of Hull2017: in my research, I observe a prominence of events dedicated to the celebration of the socio-cultural value of gender equality.

The trend has been acknowledged by multiple observing-participants in reflections on the overall programming practices of Hull2017. Vocalising the observations of several research participants, Anna highlights: "[I think] it is not a coincidence that there is a women festival, some kind of LGBT+ festival and there was a refugee event [...]" (Anna, Observing-Participant, Interview, July 2017). The presence of equality-themed events and the consequent festivalisation of equality is neither a coincidence nor an accident; rather, Anna's observation resonates with James' vision for the year-long celebration of Hull2017. The senior manager of Hull 2017 Ltd explains the programming strategy as follows:

> We did look, we did look at it constantly to make sure that [...] we were engaging everybody. And yes, then, you know, there is always an occasion and a celebration to zoom in on particular identities. So, that is why we said: "yes, we would do [the] *Women of the World* [festival]". We can and we did [the] *LGBT50* [celebrations]. [...] We staged a collection of events that everybody found connection with and more importantly nobody felt excluded from.
>
> (James, Political Actor, Interview, December 2017)

The presence of equality-themed events is not only an observation of the trained observing-participants on a quest to support the research, as an interviewed artist (Hugo, Cultural Actor, Interview, October 2017) suggests. Rather, the festivalisation of equality is pivotal to the programming strategy of the event of Hull2017.

Discussing this programming trend, research participants highlight three effects of the event-based structure for the production of cultures of gender equality. Firstly, the event dynamics are highlighted as an essential influence for the negotiations of plural notions of equality. Secondly, through the celebration of equality, residents observe a process of normalising the celebrated discourses, as the activities enable a public visibility of the socio-cultural value. The third effect is formulated as a critique, as the temporal limitations of the event-based structure seem to isolate the discourse and restrict its sustainable developments and progressions.

Energising equality

The relevance of event-based structures for the production of cultures of gender equality becomes apparent through an understanding of the energies of events, festivals and celebrations. Similar to the conceptual and empirical outlines of liminal event experiences in Chapter 2, cultural actors address festivals through dynamic, energetic characteristics. Event energies are cited as an important structural influence for the production of cultures of gender equality. As a producer of *LGBT50* for Hull 2017 Ltd, Coby synthesises:

> The energy of the festival is that you have multiple events. So, when people want to collaborate things together, they can. But not to the exclusion of other events. I think festivals are useful in that way of providing small or large events over a period of time. They offer individual voices an opportunity to express themselves either collectively or individually.
> [...]
> A festival is particularly useful because it is a diverse programme so you are giving independent stages to different voices as well as [creating] collective moments of a variety of voices to congregate.
> (Coby, Cultural Actor, Interview, October 2017)

Simultaneous happenings allow multiple actors to express their perspectives and embrace the previously discussed plurality of performances of equality. Therefore, event-based, energetic structures facilitate the production of cultures of gender equality and enable the co-existence of multiple interpretations in the celebratory context.

Normalisation of equality

Along with event energies and their invitation for the creation of plural meanings in shared space, research participants stress that event frameworks enable a normalisation of equality discourses. In her observations of the *LGBT50* celebrations, observing-participant Anna highlights that festival frameworks expose a celebratory community and normalise discourses relating to the celebrated values. She clarifies:

> Once again, probably like other events, [which] we already commented [upon], *LGBT50* had for me a little bit of this bring-stuff-to-masses element. Just like trying to slide in [the discourses and struggles for equality] in some simple and right accessible way.
> (Anna, Observing-Participant, Interview, July 2017)

Related to her previously cited observations of the narrative strategies of comfort, Anna addresses the festival framework as an important infrastructural condition to "bring-[equality]-to-masses". Her initial critique of the scrutiny of complexity for the sake of accessibility influences her observations on the normalisation of equality. However, she acknowledges and appreciates the potential reach of festival frameworks and their contribution to the normalisation of the socio-cultural values that are celebrated in the event. This normalising effect of the festivalisation of equality becomes particularly relevant regarding sensitive issues included in some investigated activities. Considering a panel on domestic violence in the *Women of the World Festival*, observing-participant Sophia argues that the festival framework allows access to information about the topic on neutral grounds:

> Was it necessary to have [the panel about domestic abuse] there [in the festival]? [...] I think it was a good opportunity. It didn't have to be there, but, because it was under the [*Women of the World*] umbrella, they had probably more chance of people attending. If it had been sort of an event, a stand-alone event, then I don't think it would have been as well attended and [it would not have received] the same audience.
>
> [...]
>
> There is also that issue to have it in the context of the larger festival, as you are not necessarily going to a domestic abuse meeting. You are going to a festival that happened to [have] a domestic abuse thing. So, you are not labelling yourself as a victim of domestic abuse. So, there is that. There is a kind of creating a space that it is ok to talk about it, because it is within this wider context of a festival.
>
> (Sophia, Observing-Participant, Interview, March 2017)

In relation to the *Women of the World Festival* and its panel discussions on domestic violence, Sophia points out that a festivalisation of equality enables new approaches to sensitive topics and political issues, while also raising awareness of the struggle towards equality. Without necessarily exposing individuals or communities as immediate victims, the festivalisation creates a platform from which engage in a more discrete manner which, in effect, is contributing to a normalisation of the subject. In agreement with Anna's and Sophia's statements, I defend the normalisation of equality discourses through the associated festivalisation trend. Through continuous efforts to celebrate socio-cultural values, cultures of gender equality become normalised in the context of Hull2017 and hopefully beyond the year-long event.

Nevertheless, the normalisation of equality discourses requires a nuanced reading. While normalising tendencies necessarily give legitimacy to the debate, they also create a hegemonic understanding of the struggles. In reflecting on the *LGBT50* celebrations, observing-participant Alex highlights this relationship:

> I do think there is this strange thing as well that actually pride is almost one of these things now, which has like (pause) I can't think of the word. (pause) It almost has like a level of legitimacy in the public. Sort of a conception on a level of like moral legitimacy. [...] [Pride] has gotten this level of authority that is almost like if you critique [its politics in regard to its militarism or consumerism], it is almost like you are homophobic.
>
> (Alex, Observing-Participant, Interview, August 2017)

Alex addresses that in the general context of LGBT+ Pride celebrations, the festivalisation of the celebrated value of equality has reached not only a normalising level but also an uncritical legitimacy and hegemony. Connected to the concept of homonationalism, as briefly addressed in the introductory chapter, the celebration of equality is affected by contradicting moralities. On the one hand, this legitimacy contributes to the production of cultures of gender equality, as normalisation processes are taking place. On the other hand, the legitimacy of these celebrations constructs a standardised discourse which, in reference to its morality, cannot be questioned. As the event and celebrated value of gender equality engrains further into national agendas, the risk of the commodification of the celebrated cultures of gender equality increases.

Isolating equality

Following the debates on the normalisation of equality based on the festivalisation of socio-cultural values, Hull2017's emphasis on celebrating cultures of gender equality in scheduled timeframes is a source of critique for its tendency to isolate the discourses. With attention to the *LGBT50* celebrations, observing-participant John's summary exemplifies the concern:

> They did this week [of *LGBT50*] where they did focus on [gender and sexual equality] and then the rest of the year, it has just been business as normal. It happened as discussed: [the event] comes; [its content] only matters during the week. [...] I did think about this for the rest of the year: for example, during the concert, *I Feel Love*, on the night, you know, they kept saying: "Oh ladies, gentlemen and those not on the gender binary". It is the only time, I heard that in

the entire year, you know they never said it in any other event. They always say: "Ladies and gentlemen". They don't say the rest of it.
(John, Observing-Participant, Focus Group, November 2017)

As John describes, during the designated time period of events, festivals and celebrations, struggles for gender equality are highlighted. However, further long-term references are missing. John's observation outlines the infrastructural conditioning that the festivalisation of equality is subject to: while the festival atmosphere is generally appreciated, research participants question what kind of cultures of gender equality are fostered if the celebration of the socio-cultural value is limited to defined, scheduled moments. The sporadic nature of the celebration of equality is perceived as a limitation to the production of cultures of gender equality. The temporal features and lack of continuations of the celebration of socio-cultural value is also critiqued by cultural actors. They share John's concerns and agree that the continuation is difficult. In the context of LGBT+ awareness, Max, a member of a charity involved in the production of *LGBT50*, not only shares these concerns but also expresses his frustration. His emotional reactions come from the lack of crossovers and collaborations between different festivals, their contents and infrastructures. He explains:

I get very frustrated with other events in the city like *Freedom [Festival]* for example. It frustrates me [how they address the notion of freedom]. Freedom is so much more than just race. It is the freedom to be yourself in all different formats and freedom is – yes – LGBT+. The pride movement is one element specifically to do with sexual orientation and gender identity, but I think that we need to get loud and get supportive with other events and there needs to be more cross-over with stuff throughout [the event schedule].
(Max, Cultural Actor, Interview, August 2017)

While a continuation of the celebration of equality is aspired to and assumed, Max experiences frustrations about the isolating effects of the festivalisation of equality. Even though events relate to one another in content and in their political aspirations, cross-overs between major equality-themed festivals in the city do not take place. John's and Max's experiences illustrate a crucial limitation to the festivalised structure of Hull2017. Both research participants address a lack of continuation. The limited time periods of festival frameworks isolate the celebrations and their contents to particular moments.

These structural restrictions correspond with considerations previously raised in Chapter 2. Addressing the encounters and dynamics of audiences with equality-themed contents, in that chapter I argue for a cautious understanding of the potential of transformative engagements and quote observing-participant Alex's question: "Where is the space for continued conversation?" (Alex, Observing-Participant, Interview, October 2017). Taking this call for continued engagement into account, the influence of the infrastructural conditions of the festivalisation of equality show an immediate effect not only on the engagement with equality-themed contents but also on the celebration of equality in general.

Materialities of in/equalities – minor aspects with major effects

In the following section, I move from the rather abstract, intangible considerations of the festivalisation of equality, to the more tangible, concrete material conditions of events, which I generically address as 'materialities'. In my conversations with observing-participants, supposedly banal aspects of event production such as the provision of food and beverages, restricted access due to security fences or alternations of bus routes kept coming up. While I initially was inclined to brush off these considerations as irrelevant for the analysis of the event-based production of cultures of gender equality, the sheer number of statements required me to take seriously these materialities of celebrations. As research participants further contemplated these material conditions in relation to their contribution to the meaning-making process, it became clear to me that these supposedly banal impressions are key influences in the infrastructural conditions fostering, negotiating and producing cultures of gender equality in event settings. As a result, I showcase how minor aspects such as bus fares or toilet facilities have a major effect on the celebration of equality. Due to repeated reflections by the majority of research participants, my analysis centres on the two prominent themes of ticketing structures and spatial arrangements as crucial examples of the material negotiation of cultures of gender equality.

Ticketing equality

My empirical research shows that the general availability of tickets and related expenses are central concerns for research participants. Already, in their first observation opportunity during the *Women of the World Festival*, various observing-participants critically commented on the ticketing structures. The festival was priced at ten pounds per day. Additionally, the opening and closing event was ticketed and required extra payment. While in other parts of the UK this price might be a bargain for a day ticket, for Hull's cultural offer, a ten-pound ticket could be considered a mid-range ticket price. Observing-participant Rachel's reaction summarises the general attitude regarding ticketing strategies, as she explains:

> I was pretty angry [and thought I had to] explode some time, because people like me [...] can't spend or don't have the spare cash to spend 10 or 15 pounds to go to [the *Women of the World Festival*].
>
> (Rachel, Observing-Participant, Interview, March 2017)

Observing-participant Sophia shares Rachel's concern and further expands on the perceived disturbance:

> [The ticketing structure is] compartmentalising different areas of society [...] in a whole range of ways. [...] Not having disposable income to be able to get [a ticket] straight away [means] [the tickets] only go to people [who] have disposable income. This ensures that the shows will only get a certain sector of society. They don't get a fair representation of everybody in the city. The system makes sure that happens, which is very sad, because it means that City of Culture is only for one group of people. And this feeds into the kind of feeling that a lot of people have: that it is not for them; that it is only for a particular community or a particular sector of the community.
>
> (Sophia, Observing-Participant, Interview, March 2017)

For Rachel and Sophia, the ticketing prices are a source of frustration and anger. Rachel's anger is reasoned in Sophia's explanation, as both participants perceive the pricing structure as an infrastructural injustice reproduced by equality-themed events. This material condition sets crucial limitations on potential audience members who have lower income levels and reduced flexibility in expenses.

Not only the expenses for tickets but also the associated booking procedures fuel experiences of injustice. It is to be noted that due to major technical difficulties in one of the first large-scale events of Hull2017, ticketing logistics were established as a core concern of research participants. Even though the initial failures in the newly installed, city-wide booking system were quickly resolved, ticketing procedures remained a source of uncertainty and insecurity throughout the entire 365 days of Hull2017. Along with her concerns regarding the exclusionary practices of ticketing prices, Sophia explains that "[the tickets were going] to the people, who can sit on technology" (Sophia, Observing-Participant, Interview, March 2017). Due to the timings of ticket releases and their online execution, she observes that "people, who have access to technology during working hours, when they go live" (Sophia, Observing-Participant, Interview, March 2017) will be able to gather tickets and therefore engage in the programmed events of Hull2017. Observing-participant Anna expands on Sophia's concerns regarding the executive barriers of online ticketing processes. Reflecting on the booking processes of *Assemble Fest,* she explains that she would be definitely interested in attending the event, however, that she "would not get tickets, if it wasn't for [the research participation], because [she] would wake up too late" (Anna, Observing-Participant, Interview, June 2017). Anna reasons her joking remark on "waking up too late" as follows:

> The way the tickets were working and the way you had to really be a very prepared and organised person to just be part of this festival – this is like a very Northern European concept: everything is accessible, if you are smart enough to look it up before; book something in advance; prepare yourself; prepare an agenda. Considering that many people aren't very smart and bright and quick [...], they would see nothing. This was the part I didn't like, because it is kind of against this value or the spirit that they wanted to bring.
> (Anna, Observing-Participant, Interview, June 2017)

The observing-participants' reflections portray that ticket prices and logistical difficulties feed into systems of exclusion and even discrimination. While Rachel and Sophia highlight exclusionary tendencies due to the affordability of tickets and related executive dilemmas of booking procedures, Anna argues further that the idea of a ticketing strategy contradicts the ethos of the celebration of equality. Several cultural and political actors participating in the research agree with the observations by observing-participants and challenge traditional booking and ticketing strategies by using alternative procedures: the usage of outdoor spaces, ticketed-but-free events, pay-as-you-wish events as well as open-access rehearsals are just a few alternative techniques addressed and appreciated by research participants.

Spaces of equality

Engaging further with the materiality of events as an infrastructural condition influencing the production of the investigated sociocultural values, I shift my focus from the ticketing structures to the spatial arrangements of equality-themed events. Firstly, I address the re-claiming of spaces and consequent visibility for equality. Secondly, I highlight particular examples such as toilet facilities and VIP spaces to discuss how these spatial arrangements facilitate or harm the event-based production of cultures of gender equality.

The selection of venues for the celebration of equality is a crucial point of discussion. In research interviews, several cultural actors took the opportunity to reason their decisions in selecting specific locations for their equality-themed events. In relation to the *Women of the World Festival* and *LGBT50*, Abbie and Henry highlight the relevance of the selected spaces for their celebration of equality. They ground their spatial decisions in their convictions to re-claim spaces for the visibility of the struggles for equality. As a member of the production team of the *Women of the World Festival*, Abbie emphasises:

> Doing [the *Women of the World Festival*] in [the] City Hall and some of the other venues was [...] very important. [...] I think it is [...] really important [that Hull2017] looked at, I suppose, not only arts and culture but also those kind of bigger political questions about our society and gave those platforms, [...] so we used this City Hall to explore these issues.
>
> (Abbie, Cultural Actor, Interview, March 2017)

Influenced by the early date of March 2017, the *Women of the World Festival* was an indoor event. The civic building, City Hall, served as the main location for the three-day celebration. Additionally, the programme integrated surrounding venues such as Ferens Art Gallery or Kingston Art Gallery through satellite activities. As Abbie suggests, the reclamation of these civic spaces had a crucial effect on the celebrated values as, symbolically and physically, equality discourses were placed in the public realm. As a member of an artists' collective involved with the production of *LGBT50*, Henry agrees with Abbie's ambition to re-claim spaces for equality and highlights the need for visibility of equality discourses. He explains:

> We decided not to be hidden away behind some buildings [...]. We wanted to be where the shoppers could see us, so they would get involved with us. We don't want an exclusive gay party [...] in a ghetto away from the ordinary people. We want to do it alongside the ordinary people [...] in the middle of a working-class town like Hull in the streets. [...] I believe in not being separate; being in a gay club. Separated away. I think that is boring.

Henry's reflections refer to the outdoor *Summer Tea Party*, the closing event of *LGBT50* in July 2017. Embracing the specificities of Queen Victoria Square with its landmark statue and podium surrounded by the majestic buildings of the Maritime History Museum, Hull City Hall and Ferens Art Gallery, visibility for the celebration of equality was guaranteed. While obviously the pre-existence of appropriate event equipment influences decisions, Abbie's and Henry's statements outline that the re-claiming of spaces is a crucial motivation in the selection of location. As acknowledged in Chapter 4 in relation to the discussion of the stories of equality, visibility is an important aspect in the celebration of equality. Ammaturo's (2016) and Browne's (2007) conceptual discussions of claiming hegemonic spaces for gendered and sexual otherness is therefore not only enacted in discursive, but also in material forms through the request for spatial visibility. The claiming of spaces and the consequent visibility that such spaces enable, is a crucial contribution to the production2 of cultures of gender equality in Hull2017.

Beyond the selection of locations, events' spatial arrangements materially condition the production of cultures of equality. Therefore, I argue that spatial features become facilitators of equality discourses. In the context of the *Women of the World Festival* and *LGBT50*, I observe spatial arrangements which have supportive and conflicting effects on the meaning-making processes of the two festivities.

For this discussion, my attention first turns to the spatial facilities as arranged in the *UK Pride Party* in Queen's Garden. Max, a member of a charity involved in the organisation of *LGBT50*, enlightens my understanding of festive spaces and facilities as he outlines the spatial concept of the event:

> We have those open spaces where people can sit down on the grass with the comfort of their family and they are encouraged to explore the space. [...] There is an area where you can get a drink. There is an area where you eat, or you can talk to people. There is even an area where you can have an HIV test. There is an area of art works. There is a band stand. I think the way that this space is set up is kind of perfect for [the *UK*] *Pride* [*Party*] because there is [space for everything].
>
> (Max, Cultural Actor, Interview, August 2017)

The cultural actor shows strong awareness of the audience's needs, which is translated into the spatial concept of the event venue. His understanding of spatial features becomes particularly clear in the provision of changing and toilet facilities. Max outlines:

Having access to [...] gender neutral facilities, where you don't have to choose, you don't have to feel awkward that I am going into the ladies or the gents, but actually I am just going into the toilet, because I am just a person who has to pee, [is so important for the event]. [Another thing is that] we have got a very strong Trans community in Hull, so we provide changing facilities.

(Max, Cultural Actor, Interview, August 2017)

In both quotations, Max clarifies the importance of spatial features and highlights that material conditions support the socio-cultural values celebrated in events. As illustrated, particularly in respect to toilet facilities, the general provision of services in designated spaces supports the celebration of equality. This supposedly simple aspect shows perfectly how the celebratory community, the celebrated content and the infrastructures of celebrations work and fit together.

While Max's spatial concept shows how material conditions can have supportive effects on the celebration of equality, I also encountered contradicting arrangements in other equality-themed events; for example: the provision of a VIP space at the *Women of the World Festival*. I turn to my own observations of the festival in order to illustrate the dispute: as I supported the *Women of the World* Circle of Friends, I received a free ticket to the opening ceremony of the festival. On the evening of the opening, while around 30 people waited already on the main plaza in front of the venue, I walked into the main foyer to pick up my ticket and was asked by a volunteer to follow her. Without having received any information about special treatment, I was taken to a back room behind the main stage, where I encountered many members of the Circle of Friends, festival performers and the team of Hull 2017 Ltd enjoying a free buffet of canapés and wine. In a short speech, Rosie Millard greeted the invited guests to the festival's opening ceremony and expressed her gratitude on behalf of the team of Hull 2017 Ltd. Observing-participant Sophia, who was with me at the time, reflected upon the arrangement:

Glamour, Glamour, Glamour. All of the sort of knows and faces in the city were there [in this VIP space], you know, all of the best people were there. [...] For all the special people, the business leaders and the special people in the city. People, who sort of exist in the top layer of the pile and not the regular folk, who had to wait outside.

(Sophia, Observing-Participant, Interview, March 2017)

As Abbie, a member of the production team of the festival, explains to me, this special treatment and the spatial segregation in the form of a VIP lounge derived from a grateful intention. However, the spatial arrangement and its mechanism of gratitude contrasts with the equality-promoting ethos of the festival. The separation of certain individuals from others as well as the special treatment of particular guests disturbed the celebration of equality that was just about to take place. While Max's conception of space facilitates the event's production of cultures of gender equality, I argue that the spatial arrangement of a VIP space in the context of the *Women of the World Festival* restricted and even harmed the supposedly celebrated value of gender equality.

Capitalising upon equality – equality discourses in the light of neoliberal commodification

In order to close the discussion of infrastructural conditions in equality-themed events, my attention turns to the economic realm, in which the celebration of equality in Hull2017 embeds. In order to understand this economic context of the production of cultures of gender equality in Hull2017, I return to the motivations of Hull's UKCOC event. As introduced through the spray-painted letters, *Change Is Happening* – further discussed in Chapter 2 – economic regenerative agendas drive the UKCOC initiative in general and the event of Hull2017 in particular. In evaluating the year-long event, the Culture, Place and Policy Institute (2019: 44) notes:

> For a city facing some of the greatest economic challenges of any in the UK, with high unemployment, the decline of older industries and large parts of the urban area being amongst the most deprived in the UK, the economic uplift that the [UKCOC] award could bring was always paramount.

In respect to tourism figures and employment data, the evaluation report highlights important key findings in relation to the outcome of Hull2017:

> The volume of tourism visits to Hull in 2017 increased by 9.7% from 2016 (from just over 5.6m to 6.2m) [...] Growth from 2012 to 2018 was about 31%. [...] Jobs in the visitor economy grew year-on-year (by just over 27%) between 2012 and 2017 (from 5297 to 6735). [...] Employment in the broader creative industries sector (which

includes the cultural sector) showed steady growth, from 1850 jobs in 2015 to 2135 in 2017 (+15.4%).

(Culture Place and Policy Institute, 2019: 48)

With attention to these numbers, the project of Hull2017 needs to be understood in its own economic regenerative parameters. Its celebration of equality cannot be extracted from the equation. Commercial interests affect not only equality-themed events but also the arts and cultural sector in general. In the context of ongoing austerity politics and associated cuts in public funding in the UK, arts, culture and events constantly seek new sources of income and forms of financial sponsorship. Therefore, the financial involvement of the private sector is continuously growing and, as Bianchini et al. (2013) suggest, is leading to the privatisation and related commercialisation of arts, culture and events.

In the previous section, I cited James, a senior manager of Hull 2017 Ltd, who addressed cultures of gender equality as a core influence for the programming strategy of the year-long celebration. While appreciative of this ambition, observing-participants call for caution in the relationship between the celebration of equality and the economic interests of Hull2017. Observing-participant Anna summarises the concern:

> We are talking about a big event [when talking about Hull2017,] involving a lot of money and looking forward to [getting] more tourists and investments. [This system is] very much established in a capitalist logic. [It seems the celebrations are] not just about building values. This is not the biggest purpose.
>
> (Anna, Observing-Participant, Interview, July 2017)

In her reflections, Anna notes that the celebration of equality in the context of Hull2017 is not just a matter of good will, but essentially engrained in the economic regenerative strategies of the event. Rather than fostering the celebrated values for a production of cultures of gender equality, the observing-participant suggests that the infrastructures serve the capitalist logic of profitability. Observing-participant Alex expands upon Anna's reflections as he explains:

> My feeling about the whole [celebration of equality] is still like: [pause] the conversation is like a capitalist production within that whole vomit-inducing system. It is just business as usual. I don't think it is part of a conversation of trying to really undercut the

roots of white supremacist imperialist capitalist heteropatriarchy. I
feel it is the opposite.

(Alex, Observing-Participant, Interview, April 2017)

For Anna and Alex, the production of cultures of gender equality
cannot be considered outside the context of their infrastructures of
existence. As both participants point out, rather than undercutting,
challenging or questioning capitalist structures, Hull2017's equality-
themed activities risk becoming a commodity within the economic
regenerative framework.

Commodifying equality

While commodifying tendencies are addressed in various equality-
themed events, the *UK Pride Parade and Party*, integrated in the
LGBT50 celebrations, is a central point of discussion in respect to the
commodification of equality discourses. As a member of a charity
involved in the production of the specific event, Max acknowledges that
tensions between political interests and infrastructural conditioning
exist. He declares: "We have got to watch out for Pride becoming commercial" (Max, Cultural Actor, Interview, August 2017). Max remarks
that various – especially bigger – LGBT+ Pride events in the UK choose
commercial approaches in order to make the event profitable to the
organisers and "balance [their efforts]" (Max, Cultural Actor, Interview,
August 2017). In the context of Hull's LGBT+ Pride event in 2017, he
shares his conviction for the need for a free event, but simultaneously
acknowledges that the event "has to be paid for" (Max, Cultural Actor,
Interview, August 2017). With a sarcastic remark, he highlights that the
celebration of equality does not "happen out of fresh air and just good
will" (Max, Cultural Actor, Interview, August 2017). Therefore, Max
calls for awareness concerning commercial trends and tendencies that
equality-themed events face.

In line with Max's sensed tension and call for awareness, several members of the team of observing-participants share their
concerns regarding an eventual commodification of equality. The *UK
Pride Parade and Party* is a crucial focal point for these concerns,
as the presence of commercial companies in the parade fuelled the
debate. Observing-participant Rosa expressed her surprise about
"the number of organisations" parading under the rainbow banner,
"who [to her knowledge] were not directly connected with the gay
movement" (Rosa, Observing-Participant, Interview, August 2017).
The observation and associated reaction are shared by numerous

observing-participants. However, rather than mere surprise, Sophia reflects upon the companies' presence in the parade with a nuance of annoyance:

> The organisations, they just marched along. It is very strange. I don't understand why they were there. They were there with their T-shirts on and whatever. The T-shirt was saying where they have come from or what their organisation was. [...] The people who were there advertising a car hire place – what was that about?
>
> (Sophia, Observing-Participant, Interview, August 2017)

Following her expression of annoyance, Sophia's lingering doubts concerning organisations' motivation for and interests in supporting the production of cultures of gender equality boils down to her pointed observation: "You don't know if they are there to support the struggle for equality, or if they want those struggling for equality to support them" (Sophia, Observing-Participant, Informal Conversation, August 2017). She clearly senses a conflict of interests in the commodification trends developing in the celebration of equality.

The observing-participants' remarks are in line with Max's experience of producing, among other LGBT+ events in Hull, the *UK Pride Parade and Party* in 2017. Pointing out that LGBT+ Pride events tend to be co-opted for organisations' interests, he illustrates the concern in relation to the application of the UK Independence Party[2] to the parade. Max explains:

> We did have applications for the parade from UKIP. We had an email from the UKIP organisation and we – our chair – went back to them on behalf of the board [and asked]: "Can we have a copy of your manifesto? Can you explain to us what your policies are with regards to supporting and helping the LGBT+ community?" Nothing came back [Pause].
>
> (Max, Cultural Actor, Interview, August 2017)

Shifting away from the involvement of private companies, Max's example highlights dynamics of commodification in relation to political parties. He expresses great awareness of the fact that the campaign for equality is highly dependent on governmental politics. Therefore, he does not dismiss the need for party political support. However, he simultaneously calls into question the motivations of political parties supporting an LGBT+ event. Regarding UKIP's interest in joining the *UK Pride Parade and Party*, Max suggests that the application might not be driven by an agenda for equality, but rather, that the presence, involvement and participation in equality discourses serves the party as a tool for attracting different segments of potential voters. In agreement with Sophia, Max explains that rather than supporting the struggle for equality, the company's, party's or institution's presence supports the organisation's image and future profitability. Hence, equality is used as a value, which can be co-opted, commodified and commercialised for the profit of its supporters.

So what? Opportunities for equality in light of infrastructural pressures

The interrogations of event infrastructures highlight that cultures of gender equality are at risk in regard to inappropriate structural conditions. In respect of the festivalisation of equality, I argued event dynamics have a normalising effect as the investigated celebrations "bring-stuff-to-masses" (Anna, Observing-Participant, Interview, July 2017). Next to these processes of normalisation, I highlighted that temporal characteristics of events eventually provoke an isolation of equality discourses as contents are singled out in a limited space-time. Regarding the material conditions of this festivalisation, I showcased, through discussions of ticketing strategies and spatial arrangements, the influence infrastructural conditions can have on the experiential accounts of the celebration of equality. Contrasting the cautious consideration of toilet facilities and the blunt VIP spatial segregation, I noted a need for awareness of these material details, as they define not only the event dynamics but also the celebrated values of the event. The negotiations of supportive and harmful infrastructural conditions are clarified by the economic regenerative ambitions that frame Hull's celebration of equality. While the investigated equality-themed events are set in a general context of economic developmental goals, Rosa, Sophia and Max observe the commodification of equality closely in regard to the vast participation of companies, organisations and institutions in the *UK Pride Parade and Party*. Max is aware that events do not "happen out of fresh air and just good will" (Max, Cultural Actor, Interview, August 2017); however, all research participants call for a close consideration of the motivations and interests of supporters.

The empirical insights in this chapter leave a large void and provoke me to ask: So What? Is the celebration of equality doomed to existing infrastructural conditions of inequalities? The analysis presented here might confirm this. The cited research participants suggest that the investigated equality-themed events are conditioned by infrastructures of inequalities. However, by borrowing arguments provided by Max, I emphasise the opportunities for learning in this circumstance:

> I think that it would be rather naive to think that Pride wasn't political, because it always has been. It is just that perhaps the political aspects of it are less obvious than they were. So, pride is a protest. Going to pride is a parade and a celebration.
>
> (Max, Cultural Actor, Interview, August 2017)

All research participants grasp that infrastructural conditions are an essential contribution to the political potential of a celebrations such as Hull2017. In placing the research participants in conversation with each other, the initial reference to Browne (2007) crystallises in the consideration of event infrastructures: negotiating the party and its politics on an infrastructural level is central to the production of cultures of gender equality in events.

Notes

1 For the purposes of clarification, I outlined the sector developments in the second half of the twentieth century in accordance with Newbold et al.'s (2015) description. As addressed in the introduction, the scholars highlight that while in the 1960s and 1970s events were framed by community-orientated, politically loaded tendencies, the event sector radically shifted in the 1990s and early 2000s and changed to become a highly professional and lucrative industrial branch characterised by commercialising and commodifying influences.
2 Further addressed as UKIP.

6 Doing gender in events

Perspectives for an eventful future

Dancing paper snippets and spray-painted brick walls

I started this book with a blast of confetti catapulted into the sky. Being showered in confetti is not only a pleasant memory of my fieldwork experience, but also inspires my thinking about the correlations between gender and events: just as colourful paper snippets dance through air to create a remarkable sight and sensation, the imbrication of the two conceptual notions generates multiple and meaningful theoretical possibilities. Situating the conceptual spectacle in the concrete empirical analysis, I followed the confetti's journey as they floated towards the brick walls of the city of Hull. Spray-painted in bright green letters, ambitions for transformation contextualise the dazzling spectacle. The theoretical possibilities of change are blasted into the air not only for the sake of their existence, but in order to embed them in the urban transformative aspirations that the city seeks in its celebration of the UKCOC title. Bringing dancing paper snippets of theoretical possibilities and spray-painted brick walls calling for change into focus, this book is a quest to understand how change is happening in the event of Hull2017 with respect to the production of cultures of gender equality.

The two metaphors playfully illustrate my argument, as this book is a plea for a gender-sensitive interpretation of events, festivals and celebrations. Thus, beyond hegemonic approaches regarding the operational or managerial analysis of festive endeavours, I argue for a nuanced reading of events: I agree with Kates's (2003: 6) suggestion to blur the boundaries of the "commercial, artistic and political arenas" of events. Additionally, I support Browne's (2007: 63) account that celebrations have to be read as "parties with politics".

This interpretation allows fruitful grounds for a gender-sensitive analysis of the politics, practices and perceptions of cultures of gender equality as fostered, produced and negotiated by Hull2017's "365 days

DOI: 10.4324/9781003121602-6

of transformative culture" (Hull2017 Ltd, 2015: 14). My in-depth analysis illustrates the socio-cultural significance of events. As a "part[y]
with politics" (Browne 2007: 63), Hull2017 is not just a tool for economic regeneration; rather, the event holds and embraces potentials to
create meaning and, in so doing, it produces cultures of gender equality.
Navigating the tension between economic ambitions, social impacts and
cultural outputs, Hull2017 expresses a socio-cultural practice in which
gender is lived, equality debated and imaginaries explored. While confetti are dancing through the sky, change is taking place – not necessarily in tearing down solid structures, but by creating experiences,
framing memories and transforming lives.

This book is based on a qualitative, ethnographic investigation of the
event of Hull2017. I used the methods of semi-structured interviews,
focus group interviews and participative observation in order to engage
with the politics and practices of events. Alongside my work with political and cultural actors as research participants, I developed a collaboration with a team of observing-participants in order to examine their
perception of the equality-themed events I investigated. Spread across
the year-long celebration, I concentrated on a selection of six so-called
equality-themed events, namely: *Women of the World Festival*, *Assemble
Fest*, *LGBT50* celebrations, *Freedom Festival* and the two exhibitions,
SKIN: Freud, Mueck and Tunick and *Hull, Portrait of a City*.

In this final chapter, I synthesise the arguments and reflect on their
relevance as provided throughout this book. Contrary to a traditional
conclusion, I close the book not with a summary of the research
implications; rather, this chapter serves as an outlook and an invitation for future research. Guided by my theoretical, methodological and
empirical journey, I recommend three crucial perspectives for future
investigations of the relationship between gender and events.

Gendered lives, politics and imaginaries – recapturing conceptual considerations

My research question *How are cultures of gender equality produced in
events?* demanded a critical engagement with the political relevance
of celebrations. Borrowing from the field of Critical Event Studies,
I approached celebrations through their socio-cultural significance
and highlighted their meaning-making potential. In my search for
a "creative [research] dynamic", Lamond and Platt's (2016: 5) critical contestation of the concept of events inspired me to interpret
celebrations through a phenomenological lens. I foregrounded that, on
the one hand, events are an experience-based condition (Getz, 2007).

On the other hand, in accordance with scholars including Falassi (1987a), Finkel (2015) and Benedict (1983), I highlighted events as practices, which mirror the structures, needs and aspirations of societies in a compromised space-time. On the basis of Falassi's (1987a: 2) suggestion, I argue that celebrations need to be understood as a product of "a series of overt values that the community recognises as essential to its ideology and worldview". As situated practices with the potential to support but also disrupt the zeitgeist of a location, events are a tool for meaning-making.

This phenomenological approach to celebrations invites further consideration of the conceptual relationship between gender and events. Newbold et al.'s (2015) summary of the evolution of events since the 1950s supports Coyle and Platt's (2015: 275) claim that "champion[ing] a particular political viewpoint [in/through events] [...] is nothing new". While, according to the scholars, events are known to promote socio-cultural values, this correlation between the party and its politics lacks substantial research. In respect to the existent literature, I outlined different approaches to the study of events through Browne's (2007) triangulation of the potential of events to influence the lived experience of gender, affect gender-sensitive politics or explore imaginaries beyond normative interpretations of gender. Within the limited scholarly literature on the relationship between gender and events, I observed increased attention towards certain celebrations, which are characterised through an interest in gender and sexuality. LGBT+ Pride events and the *Michigan Women's Music Festival* are two examples frequently addressed in this research context. In my own research on Hull2017, the selection of investigated events is no exception to this rule: I examined events that were marked as equality-themed in their content, structure or ambitions. In retrospect, I recognise the limitations of this approach and strongly encourage gender-sensitive research on alternative types of celebrations. I expand on this reflection as the first research perspective entitled: *Critical Event Studies and the Politics of Gender*.

Coming out of the shadows – Hull2017 and the (re)programming of transformative ambitions

Following the theoretical argument regarding the conceptual relationship between gender and events, in Chapter 2, I concentrated on the city of Hull and its celebration of the UKCOC title in 2017. The focus on a singular case study allowed me to analyse the production of cultures of gender in depth and enabled me to respond to the question: *How are transformative ambitions engrained in the City/Capital of Culture event framework?*

Next to the presentation of COC frameworks and their event-based urban regenerative ambitions, my interpretations of Hull2017 are strongly informed by Immler and Sakker's (2014) suggestion of the ongoing (re)programming tendencies in COC events. The scholars note that beyond formerly prominent economic regenerative interests, recent host cities increasingly invest in the potential of socio-cultural transformation through COC events. With reference to Lähdesmäki (2011, 2013a, 2013b, 2014), Boland et al. (2016) and my own research (Grabher, 2019), I exemplified how such (re)programming is taking place. With increasing acknowledgement of and interest in the socio-cultural significance, event-led meaning-making practices are emphasised in current COC events. I do not suggest that economic regenerative interests vanish due to these (re)programming tendencies; rather, I appreciate that the socio-cultural transformative potential of events is being acknowledged and explored alongside the economic dimensions of these celebrations.

Based on my observations of Hull2017, I argue that this (re)programming trend also shapes the UKCOC celebration in the city. I used the slogan, *Change Is Happening*, for a metaphorical discussion of my research interests. Beyond its figurative use, the call for change in the city finds strong resonance in Hull's intention to "com[e] out of the shadows" (Hull City Council, 2013: 4). Therefore, urban transformation is a crucial ambition and perspective for the Hull2017 project. Hull's desire for change was clearly associated with an anticipated economic revival: as cited in Chapter 4, "the economic uplift that the [UKCOC] award could bring was always paramount" (Culture Place and Policy Institute, 2019: 44). However, while transformative economic ambitions were crucial to the project, Hull2017 encompassed a wider perspective of what change can mean and incorporated (re)programming perspectives in its transformative aspirations. Existing alongside each other, economic, social and cultural dimensions of change marked the city's celebration and enabled this detailed investigation of cultures of gender equality in Hull2017.

Engagements, performances and infrastructures of equality – an analytical journey

The analysis of the production of cultures of gender equality in Hull2017 took place across three chapters. Drawing upon my collected data, I responded to the following research questions in the course of the analysis:

- How are audiences engaging with produced cultures of gender equality in the context of Hull2017?
- How are cultures of gender equality performed through the programmed activities of Hull2017?
- What kind of infrastructural arrangements accommodate the production of cultures of gender equality in the context of Hull2017?

While a focus on stakeholders strongly guided my fieldwork and data collection, the analytical process shifted my attention away from the practitioners of equality towards the practices producing cultures of gender equality in the selected events. Therefore, the analysis simultaneously drew upon the experience of political and cultural actors as well as visitors to events to interrogate how audiences engage, content performs and infrastructures condition the celebration of equality in Hull2017. Obviously, these themes continuously overlap and inform each other but, for the purpose of clarity, I discussed these issues in separate chapters.

Investigating audience engagements with equality in the experience-based condition of events, I argued that individuals and communities simultaneously shape and are shaped by events through their participation in celebrations. Referring to observing-participants such as Anna, Emma, Rachel and Sophia, I noted mono- as well as dialogical encounters with equality. Hereby, Sophia was particularly attentive to subtle forms of engagements, as illustrated in her comments on the act of clapping. Using applause as an example, I outlined how audience engagements have the potential to shape the narrative of equality presented. Furthermore, I addressed audience dynamics in the investigated equality-themed events. Strategies of inclusion matched with the overarching sensation of togetherness that marked the celebration of equality in Hull2017. Attentive to eventual echo chambers and other experiences of exclusion, I closed the first analytical chapter by raising the concerns of Alex and Daniel about the transformative potential of event engagements. The observing-participants critically questioned the efficiency of the temporally limited encounters with cultures of gender equality in festive contexts and, in Alex's words, called for a "space [to] continue [the] conversation" (Alex, Observing-Participant, Interview, October 2017).

In the second analytical theme, I concentrated on the performance and performers of equality. Through my analysis, I argued that Hull2017 and its equality-themed events did not promote a singular interpretation of what equality is or should be; rather, the investigated equality-themed events presented differing, diverging and sometimes even contradicting interpretations of the notion of equality. In order to outline this argument, I gave an overview of the different storylines of equality being told in the context of Hull2017: focusing on the *LGBT50* event series, I noted the storylines of visibility, awareness and empowerment that were emphasised through the performed contents. While these storylines captured what narratives of equality were presented, I also addressed how these stories were being told. Research participants observed entertainment and comfort as two dominant narrative strategies in the equality-themed events of Hull2017. While entertaining narrative strategies fulfilled the expectations of festival visitors, critical concerns regarding comforting strategies were raised. Several observing-participants suggested that this level of comfort risked simplifying and beautifying the struggles underlying cultures of gender equality. Next to my focus on what and how stories of equality were told in the context of Hull2017, I was attentive to the performers contributing to equality-themed events. Even though, my phenomenological interpretation of events does not pay extensive conceptual attention to the position of performers in events, observing-participants pointed out their crucial position as representatives responsible for the produced cultures of gender equality. Following the observations of three representative strategies, Daniel's question, "Why are they there?", led me to examine the performers' motivations to contribute to the celebration of equality: The majority of performers expressed that their personal experiences strongly resonated with their political interests and therefore led to their professional dedication. But even beyond their individual motivations, Max and Henry clarified that working towards cultures of gender equality is a "duty of care" (Max, Cultural Actor, Interview, August 2017) as well as an opportunity to "socially engineer" the "cultural product" (Henry, Cultural Actor, Interview, July 2017) of equality. To close the discussion regarding the performance and performers of equality, Bahar pointed out that the responsibility for equality is always a shared one: the artist clarified that due to their representative position, performers are considered to be responsible for the produced cultures of equality. However, she emphasised that, beyond the performers, it is crucial to consider the decision-makers' interests in the production of cultures of gender equality.

Bahar's consideration served as an entrance point to the third and final theme of analysis: seeking to understand the "deeper structural levels" (Alex, Observing-Participant, Focus Group, November 2017) of the investigated equality-themed events, I argued that event infrastructures fundamentally shape the celebration of equality. I explored this argument by highlighting structural conditions, which have had supportive as well as harmful effects on the celebrated values in Hull2017. As event infrastructure is a far-encompassing term, I concentrated on the festival framework, the material conditions and the economic realm of the investigated equality-themed events. Firstly, I examined how the festivalisation shapes the produced cultures of gender equality. While the events' energies greatly influence the normalisation of equality discourses, research participants highlighted that the restricted timeframe of festivals and the lack of continuity between different events have a limiting effect. Secondly, I considered how the material conditions of the event contexts influenced the production of cultures of gender equality. Thus, I examined ticketing structures and spatial arrangements as crucial indications of the negotiations of the investigated socio-cultural values. Thirdly, I considered how the economic frameworks of event productions resonate with the meaning-making practices of celebrations. In accordance with research participants, I noted that socio-cultural values of gender equality are at risk of being commodified as equality-themed events and do not escape the capitalist logic of profitability. While the previous analytical themes strongly encouraged the production of cultures of gender equality in event contexts, the analytical theme regarding infrastructures of equality painted a rather disenchanting picture. Disillusioned about the structural conditions of the event-based production of socio-cultural values in Hull2017, I agreed with Max that while awareness, caution and attention towards gender-sensitive engagements and performances exist, infrastructural conditions require extensive consideration in future event practices and research.

Don't stop me now – invitation for future research

After the synthesis of and reflections on the findings and arguments, I end this chapter with an outlook for future research in the field of gender-sensitive Event Studies. My aim in this book was to correlate the notions of gender and events and illustrate their powerful relationship through my analytical journey in the context of Hull2017's celebration of equality. I never intended this book to be exhaustive of all possible angles to think about and discuss the relationship of gender and events. On the contrary, I hope this book is an informative, inspiring and interesting source for academics as well as students to further explore the gender-sensitive and eventful realities of contemporary societies. Therefore, deriving from my conceptual, methodological and empirical thinking and writing on gender and events in the context of Hull2017, I end this book with three research recommendations.

Firstly, quite obviously, I call for further research regarding the synergies between gender and events. In order to extend and deepen the knowledge of this emerging research perspective, I propose to apply the conceptual considerations, methodological practices and analytical approaches presented here as a research lens to be applied to other event contexts. Secondly, as already addressed in my analytical discussion, I see an urgent need to foster and foreground a conceptual interpretation of event infrastructures from a Critical Event Studies perspective. In my analysis, I showcased the importance of this research perspective, as infrastructures are a core influence on the meaning-making potential of events. Thirdly and finally, the research recommendations would not be complete without an acknowledgement of the severe changes of event landscapes in 2020 due to the COVID-19 pandemic and its resultant economic crisis. In the context of these drastic transformations, I emphasise the value of and need for research in and about events, their associated communities and their celebrated values. Through a Critical Event Studies research approach, academics and students can advocate for the relevance of events and thus contribute to how celebrations can position, manage and envision themselves in what is, hopefully, an eventful future.

Research perspective 1: critical event studies and the politics of gender

My first recommendation borrows its title from a symposium, which took place at Queen Margaret University in September 2017. In this exchange, I was able to engage for the first time in my research experience with a group of academics eagerly debating the value of gender in events. While the conference title might be rather traditional, the symposium enabled me to develop my approaches to the subject matter. Beyond my own nostalgic contemplation of this conference, the title, *Critical Event Studies and the Politics of Gender*, perfectly describes my first research recommendation, as I flag the importance of gender-sensitive approaches in Event Studies and recommend that further research on the subject matter is urgently needed.

In the introduction to this book, I cited Coyle and Platt (2015), who explained that the celebration of socio-cultural values in events is nothing new; however, as my literature review indicated, a systematic analysis of gender in events is rare. Finkel et al. (2018: 1) explain: "It is only recently that issues of under-representation, marginalisation, and intolerance have begun to emerge in the critical events discourse". Therefore, I strongly agree with Dashper and Finkel's (2020:

79) suggestion that it is urgently necessary "to draw events gender researchers out from the shadows and gendered events research in from the margins of academic scholarship". In accordance with the cited scholars, I recommend that further research on gender and events is needed in order to advance the conversations between the two fields and foster their correlations.

In addition to this general recommendation, I encourage explorations of gender-sensitive meaning-making practices outside of the expected celebratory realms. As I commented in the introductory chapter of this book, current gender-sensitive event research strongly concentrates on celebrations affiliated with progressive negotiations of gender and sexuality. Including my own research in this trajectory, LGBT+ Pride events and feminist festivals are used proportionally frequently as case studies to investigate the relationship between gender and events. Contrary to this attention to gender in equality-provoking events, the enactments, promotions and productions of gender in other types of festivities spark my curiosity: how is gender addressed in rural harvest festivals? How are automotive sporting events negotiating femininities and masculinities? How are military parades projecting notions of justice and equality? In exploring other types of events without an immediate gender-sensitive character, celebrations enable a crucial insight into the plural understandings of equality in contemporary societies.

Research perspective 2: reading event infrastructures critically

Next to my call for further research on the relationship of gender and events in various celebratory contexts, my second recommendation centres on the infrastructural conditions of events and their considerations from a Critical Event Studies perspective.

In Chapter 4, I extensively showcased the relevance of this research focus. Due to strong influences on their event experiences, research participants urged me to discuss how infrastructural conditions shape the production of cultures of gender equality. While navigating slippery theoretical grounds, my empirical material showed that structural levels of events have supportive as well as harmful effects on the produced socio-cultural values of celebrations. I concluded the analysis in reference to Max, who pointed out that the political potential, the socio-cultural significance and practices of meaning-making in events are "less obvious than they were" (Max, Cultural Actor, Interview, August 2017). According to the cultural actor, the politics of the party are shifting from the participation in a parade or the performance in the street towards the infrastructural decision taken behind the scenes. The observations of research participants highlight that the structural levels of events are a crucial territory in which socio-cultural values are negotiated. In consequence, I call for further critical research on this issue.

Even though mainstream debates in Event Studies are extensively concerned with the structural processes and practices of events, their engagement with mere operational and managerial concerns is insufficient for a Critical Event Studies research agenda. Therefore, I recommend that infrastructural conditions need to be examined through a critical lens. With respect to my own inquiry of the infrastructural production of cultures of gender equality, I encourage Critical Event Studies scholars to conceptually, methodologically and empirically engage with and elaborate on event infrastructures: how do structural levels of event production contribute to the experience-based conditions of events? How do infrastructural conditions carry socio-cultural significance and facilitate meaning-making processes in events?

Research perspective 3: researching the absence of events as their presence

In my final research recommendation, I need to acknowledge the drastic changes in the event landscape in 2020 due to the COVID-19 pandemic. Rather than a pointed recommendation, this third research perspective invites considerations, reflections and speculations on the relevance of Critical Event research in (post-)pandemic circumstances.

For clarification: in December 2019, I completed the research which informs this book. At this point, I would have been tempted to exclaim in some exaggerated form that events are omnipresent, shaping our regular lives and daily experiences, giving a relief and distraction to normality. However, with the experience of the global outbreak of COVID-19, this exclamation has lost its meaning. In 2020, the UK underwent three periods of national lockdowns and various scales of further measurements in order to stop the spread of the viral infection. In the light of these dramatic developments, the event sector has been affected massively. Some festivals explored new digital opportunities; some chose to postpone their programme to a post-pandemic time; others were completely cancelled. In summary, 2020 has been marked as a year without events – or at least without events as they used to be. In the UK, the highly lucrative event sector has struggled immensely not only in terms of the losses in its capacities to celebrate, but also in regard to the recognition of its value through the government's national funding support schemes. Campaigns such as, *We Make Events*, demand attention for and acknowledgement of the sector as a political tool, practical intervention and perceptive need (Hann, 2020). Navigating a precarious presence and uncertain future(s), the events sector and its workers are immensely impacted by this economic crisis, social deprivation and cultural void.

In light of this difficult situation, I see an urgent need to raise awareness of the value of events, their affiliated workers and associated communities. Therefore, I recommend/encourage/urge that this crucial period of drastic change needs to be made an important point in the research agenda in Critical as well as mainstream Event Studies. Many questions arise in regard to the economic and social effects that the lack of events might promote. But from a Critical Event Studies perspective, I foreground – once again – the socio-cultural significance and meaning-making potential of events. What happens to socio-cultural values when they can no longer be celebrated in the form of events?

In the postponement and consequential void of celebrations, a crucial research perspective opens that actually invites us to study the importance of events.

In this book, I hope to have raised awareness of the theoretical possibilities of the relationship between gender and events. As processes of meaning-making and therefore of socio-cultural significance, I discussed events as "parties with politics" (Browne, 2007: 63) and showcased how gender can be understood in and through events. As the investigated festivities embed in strong ambitions for change, I regarded how audiences engage with, artists produce and infrastructures condition the celebration of equality in "365 days of transformative culture" (Hull 2017 Ltd, 2015: 14) in the city of Hull. Closing the book in reference to three research recommendations, I return to the inspiration as outlined in the introduction: I throw confetti up in the air and am curious where the snippets of colourful paper might land.

References

Abrahams, R. (1987). An American vocabulary of celebrations. In A. Falassi (Ed.), *Time out of time: Essays on the festival* (pp. 173–183). University of New Mexico Press.

Aiello, G. & Thurlow, C. (2010). Symbolic capitals: Visual discourse and intercultural exchange in the European Capital of Culture Scheme. *Language & Intercultural Communication*, 6(2), 148–162. https://doi.org/10.2167/laic234.0

Åkerlund, U. & Müller, D. (2012). Implementing tourism events: The discourses of Umeå's bid for European Capital of Culture 2014. *Scandinavian Journal of Hospitality and Tourism*, 12(2), 164–180. https://doi.org/10.1080/15022250.2011.647418

Ammaturo, F. (2016). Spaces of pride: A visual ethnography of gay pride parades in Italy and the United Kingdom. *Social Movement Studies*, 15(1), 19–40. https://doi.org/10.1080/14742837.2015.1060156

Baker, C. (2015). Introduction: Gender and geopolitics in the Eurovision Song Contest. *Contemporary Southeastern Europe*, 2(1), 74–93.

Baker, C. (2017). The "gay Olympics"? The Eurovision Song Contest and the politics of LGBT/European belonging. *European Journal of International Relations*, 23(1), 97–121. https://doi.org/10.1177/1354066116633278

Baker, C. (2019). "If love was a crime, we would be criminals": The Eurovision Song Contest and the queer international politics of flags. In J. Kalman, B. Wellings & K. Jacotine (Eds.), *Eurovisions: Identity and the international politics of the Eurovision Song Contest since 1956* (pp. 175–200). Palgrave Macmillan.

Bartie, A. (2013). Introduction. In A. Bartie (Ed.), *The Edinburgh Festivals: Culture and society in post-war Britain* (pp. 1–22). Edinburgh University Press.

Benedict, B. (1983). *The anthropology of World's Fairs: San Francisco's Panama Pacific International Exposition of 1915*. Scolar Press.

Bergsgard, N. & Vassenden, A. (2011). The legacy of Stavanger as Capital of Culture in Europe 2008: Watershed or puff of wind? *International Journal of Cultural Policy*, 17(3), 301–320. https://doi.org/10.1080/10286632.2010.493214

Berlins, M. (2007, September 12). *Can applause really replace the minute's silence?* www.theguardian.com/commentisfree/2007/sep/12/comment.comment2

Bernstein Sycamore, M. (2004). *That's revolting! Queer strategies for resisting assimilation.* Soft Skull Press.

Bianchini, F. & Tommarchi, E. (2020). Urban activism and the rethinking of city cultural policies in Europe. In M. Wimmer (Ed.), *Kann Kultur Politik? – Kann Politik Kultur? Warum wir wieder mehr über Kulturpolitik sprechen sollten* (pp. 156–167). De Gruyter.

Bianchini, F., Albano, R. & Bollo, A. (2013). The regenerative impacts of European City and Capital of Culture events. In M. Leary & J. McCarthy (Eds.), *Companion to urban regeneration* (pp. 515–526). Routledge.

Black, D. (2007). The symbolic politics of sport mega-events: 2010 in comparative perspective. *Politikon: South African Journal of Political Studies*, 34(3), 261–276. https://doi.org/10.1080/02589340801962536

Boland, P. (2010). "Capital of Culture – you must be having a laugh!" Challenging the official rhetoric of Liverpool as the 2008 European Cultural Capital. *Social & Cultural Geography*, 11(7), 627–645. https://doi.org/10.1080/14649365.2010.508562

Boland, P., Mullan, L. & Murtagh, B. (2018). Young people in a city of culture: "Ultimate beneficiaries" or "Economic migrants"? *Journal of Youth Studies*, 21(2), 178–202. https://doi.org/10.1080/13676261.2017.1358810

Boland, P., Murtagh, B. & Shirlow, P. (2016). Fashioning a City of Culture: "Life and place changing" or "12-month party"? *International Journal of Cultural Policy*, 25(2), 1–20. https://doi.org/10.1080/10286632.2016.1231181

Brewster, M., Connell, J. & Page, S. (2009). The Scottish Highland Games: Evolution, development and role as a community event. *Current Issues in Tourism*, 12(3), 271–293. https://doi.org/10.1080/13683500802389730

Browne, K. (2007). A party with politics? (Re)making LGBTQ Pride spaces in Dublin and Brighton. *Social & Cultural Geography*, 8(1), 63–87. https://doi.org/10.1080/14649360701251817

Browne, K. (2009). Naked and dirty: Rethinking (not) attending festivals. *Journal of Tourism and Cultural Change*, 7(2), 115–132. https://doi.org/10.1080/14766820903033666

Browne, K. (2011). Beyond rural idylls: Imperfect lesbian utopias at Michigan Womyn's Music Festival. *Journal of Rural Studies*, 27(1), 13–23. https://doi.org/10.1016/j.jrurstud.2010.08.001

Bunnell, T. (2008). Multiculturalism's regeneration: Celebrating Merdeka (Malaysian independence) in a European Capital of Culture. *Transactions of the Institute of British Geographers*, 33(2), 251–267. www.jstor.org/stable/30133360

Byrne, M. (1987). Nazi Festival: The 1936 Berlin Olympics. In A. Falassi (Ed.), *Time out of time: Essays on the festival* (pp. 107–122). University of New Mexico Press.

Campbell, P. (2011). Creative industries in a European Capital of Culture. *International Journal of Cultural Policy*, 17(5), 510–522. https://doi.org/10.1080/10286632.2010.543461

Carniel, J. (2015). Skirting the issue: Finding queer and geopolitical belonging at the Eurovision Song Contest. *Contemporary Southeastern Europe*, 2(1), 136–154.

Cohen, A. (1980). Drama and politics in the development of London Carnival. *Man New Series*, 15(1), 65–87. https://doi.org/10.2307/2802003

Cohen, C. (1998). "This is De Test": Festival and the cultural politics of nation building in the British Virgin Islands. *American Ethnologist*, 25(2), 189–214. https://doi.org/10.1525/ae.1998.25.2.189

Cohen, S. (2013). Musical memory, heritage and local identity: Remembering the popular music past in a European Capital of Culture. *International Journal of Cultural Policy*, 19(5), 576–594. https://doi.org/10.1080/10286632.2012.676641

Costa, X. (2002). Festive identity: Personal and collective identity in the Fire Carnival of the "Fallas" (Valencia, Spain). *Social Identities*, 8(2), 321–345. https://doi.org/10.1080/13504630220151593

Coyle, T. & Platt, L. (2015). Feminist politics in the festival space. In J. Mair (Ed.), *The Routledge handbook of festivals* (pp. 273–282). Routledge.

Cudny, W. (2016). *Festivalisation of urban spaces: Factors, processes and effects.* Springer International Publishing.

Culture Place and Policy Institute. (2018). *Cultural transformations: The impacts of Hull UK City of Culture 2017*. University of Hull.

Culture Place and Policy Institute. (2019). *Cultural transformations: The impacts of Hull UK City of Culture 2017. Main evaluation findings and reflections.* University of Hull.

Cvetkovich, A. & Wahng, S. (2001). Don't stop the music: Roundtable discussion with workers from the Michigan Womyn's Music Festival. *Journal of Lesbian and Gay Studies*, 7(1), 131–151.

Dashper, K. & Finkel, R. (2020). "Doing gender" in Critical Event Studies: A dual agenda for research. *International Journal of Event and Festival Management*, 12(1), 70–84. https://doi.org/10.1108/IJEFM-03-2020-0014

Department for Culture Media and Sports. (2013). *UK City of Culture 2017: Guidance for Bidding Cities.* UK Government.

Devlin, P. (2016). City of Culture/Memory: Derry/Londonderry, 2013. In D. O'Rawe & M. Phelan (Eds.), *Post-conflict performance, film and visual arts: Cities of memory* (pp. 169–192). Contemporary Performance InterActions.

Dragićević, V., Bole, D., Bučić, A. & Prodanović, A. (2015). European Capital of Culture: Residents' perception of social benefits and costs – Maribor 2012 case study. *Acta Geographica Slovenica*, 55(2), 283–302. https://doi.org/10.3986/ags.747

Dragoman, D. (2008). National identity and Europeanization in post-communist Romania: The meaning of citizenship in Sibiu: European Capital of Culture 2007. *Communist and Post-Communist Studies*, 41(1), 63–78. https://doi.org/10.1016/j.postcomstud.2007.12.004

Eder, D., Staggenborg, S. & Sudderth, L. (1995). The National Women's Music Festival: Collective identity and diversity in a lesbian-feminist community.

Journal of Contemporary Ethnography, 23(4), 485–515. https://doi.org/10.1177/089124195023004004

European Commission. (2009). *European Capitals of Culture: The road to success from 1985 to 2010*. European Commission.

European Commission. (2010). *Summary of the European Commission conference "Celebrating 25 years of European Capitals of Culture"*. European Commission.

European Commission. (2015). *European Capitals of Culture: 30 years*. European Commission.

European Institute for Gender Equality. (2021, March 3). *United Kingdom*. https://eige.europa.eu/gender-mainstreaming/countries/united-kingdom

Falassi, A. (1987a). Festival: Definition and morphology. In A. Falassi (Ed.), *Time out of time: Essays on the festival* (pp. 1–13). University of New Mexico Press.

Falassi, A. (1987b). *Time out of time: Essays on the festival*. University of New Mexico Press.

Falk, M. & Hagsten, E. (2017). Measuring the impact of the European Capital of Culture programme on overnight stays: Evidence for the last two decades. *European Planning Studies*, 25(12), 2175–2191. https://doi.org/10.1080/09654313.2017.1349738

Finkel, R. (2009). A picture of the contemporary combined arts festival landscape. *Cultural Trends*, 18(1), 3–21. https://doi.org/10.1080/09548960802651195

Finkel, R. (2015). Introduction to special issue on social justice and events-related policy. *Journal of Policy Research in Tourism, Leisure and Events*, 7(3), 217–219. https://doi.org/10.1080/19407963.2014.995905

Finkel, R., Sharp, B. & Sweeney, M. (2018). Introduction. In R. Finkel, B. Sharp & M. Sweeney (Eds.), *Accessibility, inclusion and diversity in critical event studies* (pp. 1–5). Routledge.

Fitjar, R., Rommetvedt, H. & Berg, C. (2013). European Capitals of Culture: Elitism or inclusion? The case of Stavanger2008. *International Journal of Cultural Policy*, 19(1), 63–83. https://doi.org/10.1080/10286632.2011.600755

Fitzpatrick, S. (2010). *Rethinking the public sphere: Creativity, power and language in Liverpool's capital of culture year* [Unpublished doctoral dissertation]. The Manchester Metropolitan University.

Freedom Festival Trust. (2019, June 8). *Freedom Festival*. www.freedomfestival.co.uk/our-work/freedom-festival/

Frost, N. (2015). Anthropology and festivals: Festival ecologies. *Ethnos*, 81(4), 569–583. https://doi.org/10.1080/00141844.2014.989875

García, B. & Cox, T. (2013). *European Capitals of Culture: Success strategies and long-term effects*. European Parliament.

Gehrels, S. & Landen, T. (2015). Hotel quality in the European Capital of Culture: Leeuwarden 2018. *Research in Hospitality Management*, 5(2), 153–159. https://doi.org/10.1080/22243534.2015.11828340

Getz, D. (2007). *Event studies: Theory, research and policy for planned events*. Elsevier.

Giovanangeli, A. (2015). Marseille, European Capital of Culture 2013 ins and offs: A case for rethinking the effects of large-scale cultural initiatives. *French Cultural Studies*, 26(3), 302–316. https://doi.org/10.1177/09571558 15587236

Gorokhov, V. (2015). Forward Russia! Sports mega-events as a venue for building national identity. *Nationalities Papers*, 43(2), 267–282. https://doi. org/10.1080/00905992.2014.998043

Goulding, C. & Saren, M. (2009). Performing identity: An analysis of gender expressions at the Whitby Goth Festival. *Consumption, Markets & Culture*, 12(1), 27–46. https://doi.org/10.1080/10253860802560813

Grabher, B. (2018). Observing through participants: The analytical and practical potential of citizens' involvement in event research. *Studies on Home and Community Science*, 11(2), 66–76. https://doi.org/10.1080/09737189. 2017.1420389

Grabher, B. (2019). *Gendering Cities of Culture: City/ Capital of Culture mega-events and the potential for gender equality* [Unpublished doctoral dissertation]. University of Hull/ University of Oviedo.

Grabher, B. (2020). The privilege of subversion: Reading experiences of LGBT-themed events during Hull UK City of Culture 2017 through liminality. In I. Lamond & J. Moss (Eds.), *Liminality and Critical Event Studies: Boundaries, borders, and contestation* (pp. 79–98). Palgrave Macmillan.

Green, S. (2017). *Capitals of Culture: An introductory survey of a worldwide activity*. Prasino.

Griffiths, R. (2006). City/culture discourses: Evidence from the competition to select the European Capital of Culture 2008. *European Planning Studies*, 14(4), 415–430. https://doi.org/10.1080/09654310500421048

Hahm, J., Ro, H. & Olson, E. (2018). Sense of belonging to a lesbian, gay, bisexual, and transgender event: The examination of affective bond and collective self-esteem. *Journal of Travel and Tourism Marketing*, 35(2), 244–256. https://doi.org/10.1080/10548408.2017.1357519

Hall, C. (1989). The definition and analysis of hallmark tourist events. *GeoJournal*, 19(3), 263–268. https://doi.org/10.1007/BF00454570

Halperin, D. & Traub, V. (2009). *Gay Shame*. University of Chicago Press.

Hann, M. (2020, August 15). *"I feel like I'm failing at life": The terrible plight of music event staff*. www.theguardian.com/music/2020/aug/15/the-terrible-plight-of-music-event-staff-coronavirus-pandemic

Haraway, D. (1988). Situated knowledges: The science question in feminism and the privilege of partial perspective. *Feminist Studies*, 14(3), 575–599. https://doi.org/10.2307/3178066

Harding, S. (1987a). Conclusion: Epistemological questions. In S. Harding (Ed.), *Feminism and methodology: Social science issues* (pp. 181–191). Indiana University Press.

Harding, S. (1987b). Introduction: Is there a feminist method? In S. Harding (Ed.), *Feminism and methodology: Social science issues* (pp. 1–15). Indiana University Press.

Harding, S. (1993). Rethinking standpoint epistemology: What is "strong objectivity"? In L. Alcoff & E. Potter (Eds.), *Feminist epistemologies* (pp. 49–82). Routledge.

Herrero, L., Sanz, J., Devesa, M., Bedate, A. & José, M. (2006). The economic impact of cultural events: A case-study of Salamanca 2002, European Capital of Culture. *European Urban and Regional Studies*, 13(1), 41–57. https://doi.org/10.1177/0969776406058946

Hirsh, E., Olson, G. & Harding, S. (1995). Starting from marginalized lives: A conversation with Sandra Harding. *JAC: A Journal of Composition Theory*, 15(2), 193–225. www.jstor.org/stable/20866024

Hlavajova, M. (2017). *Art in the time of interregnum*. BAK – Basis voor aktuelle Kunst.

Holvino, E. (2010). Intersections: The simultaneity of race, gender and class in organization studies. *Gender, Work & Organization*, 17(3), 248–277. https://doi.org/10.1111/j.1468-0432.2008.00400.x

Hudec, O. & Džupka, P. (2016). Culture-led regeneration through the young generation: Košice as the European Capital of Culture. *European Urban and Regional Studies*, 23(3), 531–538. https://doi.org/10.1177/0969776414528724

Hughes, H., Allen, D. & Wasik, D. (2003). The significance of European "Capital of Culture" for tourism and culture: The case of Kraków 2000. *International Journal of Arts Management*, 5(3), 12–23. www.jstor.org/stable/41064794

Hull 2017 Ltd. (2015). *Hull UK City of Culture 2017: Strategic business plan 2015–2018*. Hull 2017 Ltd.

Hull 2017 Ltd. (2017, July 26). *LGBT50*. www.hull2017.co.uk/whatson/events/lgbt-50/

Hull City Council. (2013). *UK City of Culture 2017: Final bid*. Hull City Council.

Hull City Council. (2019, April 6). *History of Hull*. www.hullcc.gov.uk/portal/page?_pageid=221,148379&_dad=portal&_schema=PORTAL#

Hunter-Jones, P. & Warnaby, G. (2009). *Student perceptions of the European Capital of Culture: University choice and Liverpool 08*. University of Liverpool.

Immler, N. & Sakkers, H. (2014). (Re)programming Europe: European Capitals of Culture: Rethinking the role of culture. *Journal of European Studies*, 44(1), 3–29. https://doi.org/10.1177/0047244113515567

Ingram, M. (2010). Promoting Europe through "Unity in Diversity": Avignon as European Capital of Culture in 2000. *Journal of the Society for the Anthropology of Europe*, 10(1), 14–25. https://doi.org/10.1111/j.1556-5823.2010.00003.x

Iordanova-Krasteva, E., Wickens, E. & Bakir, A. (2010). Ambiguous image of Linz: Linz09 – European Capital of Culture. *Pasos: Journal of Tourism and Cultural Heritage*, 8(3), 27–37.

Johnson, K. & Up Helly Aa for Aa. (2019). Fuel for the fire: Tradition and the gender controversy in Lerwick's Up Helly Aa. *Scottish Affairs*, 28(4), 459–474. https://doi.org/10.3366/scot.2019.0298

Johnston, L. (2007). Mobilizing pride/shame: Lesbians, tourism and parades. *Social & Cultural Geography*, 8(1), 29–45. https://doi.org/10.1080/14649360 701251528

Jones, C. (2010). Playing at the queer edges. *Leisure Studies*, 29(3), 269–287. https://doi.org/10.1080/02614360903401935

Kates, S. (2003). Producing and consuming gendered representations: An interpretation of the Sydney Gay and Lesbian Mardi Gras. *Consumption, Markets & Culture*, 6(1), 5–22. https://doi.org/10.1080/10253860302699

Kates, S. & Belk, R. (2001). The meanings of Lesbian and Gay Pride Day: Resistance through consumption and resistance to consumption. *Journal of Contemporary Ethnography*, 30(4), 392–429. https://doi.org/https://doi.org/ 10.1177/089124101030004003

Kendall, L. (2006). *From the liminal to the land: Building Amazon culture at the Michigan Womyn's Music Festival* [Unpublished doctoral dissertation]. University of Maryland.

Kenttamaa Squires, K. (2019). Rethinking the homonormative? Lesbian and Hispanic Pride events and the uneven geographies of commoditized identities. *Social & Cultural Geography*, 20(3), 1–20. https://doi.org/10.1080/ 14649365.2017.1362584

Kluge, F. (2011). *Etymologisches Wörterbuch der deutschen Sprache*. De Gruyter.

Lähdesmäki, T. (2011). European Capitals of Culture as cultural meeting places: Strategies of representing cultural diversity. *Nordisk Kulturpolitisk Tidskrift*, 13(1), 27–42.

Lähdesmäki, T. (2013a). Cultural activism as a counter-discourse to the European Capital of Culture programme: The case of Turku 2011. *European Journal of Cultural Studies*, 16(5), 598–619. https://doi.org/http://dx.doi.org/ 10.1177/1367549413491720

Lähdesmäki, T. (2013b). Identity politics of the European Capital of Culture initiative and the audience reception of cultural events compared. *Nordisk Kulturpolitisk Tidskrift*, 16(2), 340–365.

Lähdesmäki, T. (2014). Discourses of Europeanness in the reception of the European Capital of Culture events: The case of Pécs 2010. *European Urban and Regional Studies*, 21(2), 191–205. https://doi.org/10.1177/0969776412448092

Lamond, I. & Platt, L. (2016). Introduction. In I. Lamond & L. Platt (Eds.), *Critical Event Studies: Approaches to research* (pp. 1–15). Palgrave Macmillan.

Leong, L. (2001). Consuming the nation: National day parades in Singapore. *New Zealand Journal of Asian Studies*, 3(2), 5–16.

Love, H. (2007). *Feeling backward: Loss and the politics of queer history*. Harvard University Press.

Luongo, M. (2002). Rome's World Pride: Making the eternal city an international gay tourism destination. *GLQ: A Journal of Lesbian and Gay Studies*, 8(1), 167–181. https://doi.org/10.1215/10642684-8-1-2-167

Mann, R., Faria, J., Sumpter, D. & Krause, J. (2013). The dynamics of audience applause. *Journal of the Royal Society Interface*, 10(85), 1–7. https://doi.org/ 10.1098/rsif.2013.0466

Markwell, K. (2002). Mardi Gras tourism and the construction of Sydney as an international gay and lesbian city. *GLQ: A Journal of Lesbian and Gay Studies*, 8(1), 81–99. https://doi.org/10.1215/10642684-8-1-2-81

Markwell, K. & Waitt, G. (2009). Festivals, space and sexuality: Gay pride in Australia. *Tourism Geographies*, 11(2), 143–168. https://doi.org/10.1080/14616680902827092

Markwell, K. & Waitt, G. (2013). Events and sexualities. In R. Finkel, D. McGillivray, G. McPherson & P. Robinson (Eds.), *Research themes for events* (pp. 57–68). CAB International.

Matarasso, F. (2018). *The normalization of participatory art* (Conference Presentation). Sharing the Legacy – Valletta European Capital of Culture 2018, Valletta, Malta.

Mayring, P. (1991). Qualitative Inhaltsanalyse. In U. Flick, E. Kardoff, H. Keupp, L. Rosenstiel & S. Wolff (Eds.), *Handbuch qualitative Forschung: Grundlagen, Konzepte, Methoden und Anwendungen* (pp. 209–213). Beltz – Psychologie Verlag Union.

McCartney, G. & Osti, L. (2007). From cultural events to sport events: A case study of cultural authenticity in the Dragon Boat Races. *Journal of Sport & Tourism*, 12(1), 25–40. https://doi.org/10.1080/14775080701496750

Mies, M. (1983). Towards a methodology for feminist research. In G. Bowles & R. Klein (Eds.), *Theories of women's studies* (pp. 117–139). Routledge.

Morris, B. (2005). Negotiating lesbian worlds: Festival communities. In *Journal of Lesbian Studies*, 9(1–2), 55–62. https://doi.org/10.1300/J155v09n01_05

Moulaert, F., Demuynck, H. & Nussbaumer, J. (2004). Urban renaissance: From physical beautification to social empowerment. *City*, 8(2), 229–235. https://doi.org/10.1080/1360481042000242175

Newbold, C., Jordan, J., Bianchini, F. & Maughan, C. (2015). Introduction: Focusing on festivals. In C. Newbold, C. Maughan, J. Jordan & F. Bianchini (Eds.), *Focus on festivals: Contemporary European case studies and perspectives* (pp. xv–xxvi). Goodfellow.

O'Callaghan, C. (2012). Urban anxieties and creative tensions in the European Capital of Culture 2005: "It couldn't just be about Cork, like". *International Journal of Cultural Policy*, 18(2), 185–204. https://doi.org/10.1080/10286632.2011.567331

O'Callaghan, C. & Linehan, D. (2007). Identity, politics and conflict in dockland development in Cork, Ireland: European Capital of Culture 2005. *Cities*, 24(4), 311–323. https://doi.org/10.1016/j.cities.2007.01.006

Office for National Statistics. (2019, May). *MYE2: Population estimates: Persons by single year of age and sex for local authorities in the UK*, mid-2019. www.ons.gov.uk/peoplepopulationandcommunity/populationandmigration/populationestimates/datasets/populationestimatesforukenglandandwalesscotlandandnorthernireland

Patel, K. (2013). *The cultural politics of Europe: European Capitals of Culture and European Union since 1980*. Routledge.

Pielichaty, H. (2015). Festival space: Gender, liminality and the carnivalesque. *Journal of Event and Festival Management*, 6(3), 235–250. https://doi.org/10.1108/IJEFM-02-2015-0009

Platt, L. & Finkel, R. (2018). Editorial. *Journal of Policy Research in Tourism, Leisure and Events*, 10(2), 113–116. https://doi.org/10.1080/19407963.2018.1418707

Ploner, J. & Jones, L. (2019). Learning to belong? "Culture" and "place making" among children and young people in Hull, UK City of Culture 2017. *Children's Geographies*, 1–14. https://doi.org/10.1080/14733285.2019.1634245

Puar, J. (2013). Rethinking homonationalism. *International Journal of Middle East Studies*, 45(2), 336–339. https://doi.org/10.1017/S002074381300007X

Quinn, B. (2003). Symbols, practices and myth-making: Cultural perspectives on the Wexford Festival Opera. *Tourism Geographies*, 5(3), 329–349. https://doi.org/10.1080/14616680309710

Quinn, B. (2009). The European Capital of Culture initiative and cultural legacy: An analysis of the cultural sector in the aftermath of Cork 2005. *Event Management*, 13(4), 249–264. https://doi.org/10.3727/152599510X12621081189077

Redmond, P. (2009). *UK City of Culture: Vision statement*. Department for Culture Media and Sports.

Richards, G. & Wilson, J. (2006). Developing creativity in tourist experiences: A solution to the serial reproduction of culture? *Tourism Management*, 27(6), 1209–1223. https://doi.org/10.1016/j.tourman.2005.06.002

Sassatelli, M. (2002). Imagined Europe: The shaping of a European cultural identity through EU cultural policy. *European Journal of Social Theory*, 5(4), 435–451. https://doi.org/10.1177/136843102760513848

Sassatelli, M. (2008). European cultural space in the European Cities of Culture: Europeanization and cultural policy. *European Societies*, 10(2), 225–245. https://doi.org/10.1080/14616690701835311

Sassatelli, M. (2009). *Becoming Europeans: Cultural identity and cultural policies*. Palgrave Macmillan.

Taylor, J. (2014). Festivalizing sexualities: Discourses of "Pride", counter-discourses of "Shame". In A. Bennett, J. Taylor & I. Woodward (Eds.), *The Festivalization of Culture* (pp. 27–48). Ashgate Publishing Group.

The European Parliament and the Council of the European Union. (2006). DECISION No 1622/2006/EC: Community action for the European Capital of Culture event for the years 2007 to 2019. *Official Journal of the European Union*, L 304(1), 1–6.

The European Parliament and the Council of the European Union. (2014). DECISION No 445/2014/EU: Union action for the European Capitals of Culture for the years 2020 to 2033 and repealing Decision No 1622/2006/EC. *Official Journal of the European Union*, L132(1), 1–12.

Tokofsky, P. (1999). Masking gender: A German carnival custom. *Western Folklore*, 58(3/4), 299–318. https://doi.org/10.2307/1500463

Tucker, M. (2008). The cultural production of cities: Rhetoric or reality? Lessons from Glasgow. *Journal of Retail and Leisure Property*, 7(1), 21–33. https://doi.org/10.1057/palgrave.rlp.5100083

Turner, E. (2008). Exploring the work of Victor Turner: Liminality and its later implications. *Suomen Antropologi: Journal of the Finnish Anthropological Society*, 33(4), 26–44.

Turner, E. (2012). *Communitas: The anthropology of joy*. Palgrave Macmillan.

Turner, V. (1969). *The ritual process: Structure and anti-structure*. Aldine.

Turner, V. (1974). Liminal to liminoid, in play, flow, and ritual: An essay in comparative symbology. *The Rice University Studies*, 60(3), 53–92. https://doi.org/1911/63159

Turner, V. (1982). Introduction. In V. Turner (Ed.), *Celebrations: Studies in festivity and ritual* (pp. 11–33). Smithsonian Institution Press.

Turner, V. (1987a). Betwixt and between: The liminal period in rites of passage. In V. Turner (Ed.), *Betwixt and between: Patterns of masculine and feminine Initiation* (pp. 3–19). Open Court Publishing Company.

Turner, V. (1987b). Carnival, ritual and play in Rio de Janeiro. In A. Falassi (Ed.), *Time out of time: Essays on the festival* (pp. 74–90). University of New Mexico Press.

Turner, V. (1989). Liminality and communitas. In V. Turner (Ed.), *The ritual process: Structure and anti-structure* (pp. 358–374). Routledge.

Umney, C. & Symon, G. (2019). Creative placemaking and the cultural projectariat: artistic work in the wake of Hull City of Culture 2017. *Capital and Class*, 1–21. https://doi.org/10.1177/0309816819884699

Voicescu, C. (2012). Conceptualization of the instrumental interpretative act for performing high-quality music. *Bulletin of Transilvania University of Brasov*, 5(2), 47–52.

Waitt, G. & Gorman-Murray, A. (2008). Camp in the country: Re-negotiating sexuality and gender through a rural lesbian and gay festival. *Journal of Tourism and Cultural Change*, 6(3), 185–207. https://doi.org/10.1080/14766820802647616

Waitt, G. & Stapel, C. (2011). "Fornicating on floats"? The cultural politics of the Sydney Mardi Gras Parade beyond the metropolis. *Leisure Studies*, 30(2), 197–216. https://doi.org/10.1080/02614367.2010.509445

Ware, C. (2001). Anything to act crazy: Cajun women and Mardi Gras disguise. *Journal of American Folklore*, 114(452), 225–247. https://doi.org/10.2307/542097

West, C. & Zimmerman, D. (1987). Doing gender. *Gender and Society*, 1(2), 125–151.

West, H. & Scott-Samuel, A. (2010). Creative potential: Mental well-being impact assessment of the Liverpool 2008 European Capital of Culture programme. *Public Health*, 124(4), 198–205. https://doi.org/10.1016/j.puhe.2010.01.012

Žilič-Fišer, S. & Erjavec, K. (2017). The political impact of the European Capital of Culture: "Maribor 2012 gave us the power to change the regime". *International Journal of Cultural Policy*, 23(5), 581–596. https://doi.org/10.1080/10286632.2015.1084299

Index

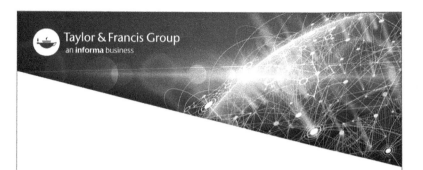

Printed in the USA
CPSIA information can be obtained
at www.ICGtesting.com
LVHW081951081123
763418LV00004B/390